India, Pakistan, and the West

India, Pakistan, and the West

PERCIVAL SPEAR

FOURTH EDITION

OXFORD UNIVERSITY PRESS

LONDON   OXFORD   NEW YORK

Contents

India and Pakistan

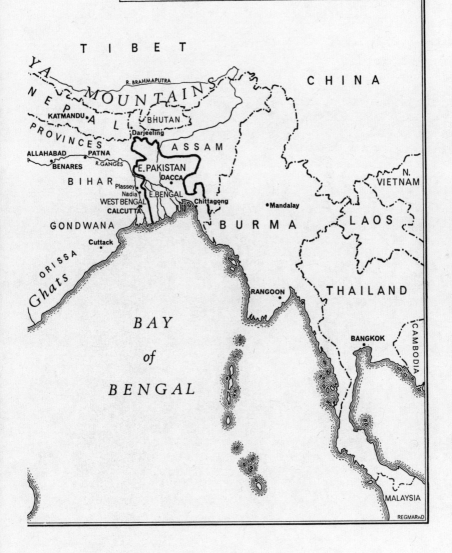

Foreword

THE WORD 'INDIA' has necessarily been used in an ambiguous sense in this book. As applied to the past, it denotes the geographical sub-continent. As applied to the present, it denotes the Indian Dominion when used in a political sense, and again the sub-continent when used geographically. No acceptable hybrid covering the whole geographical area has yet found currency and some confusion of terminology is therefore inevitable.

I should like to acknowledge the great help and encouragement received in various ways in preparing this book from the following: my wife, the late Sir Frank Noyce, Dr. R. B. Whitehead, and Mr. Guy Wint.

PERCIVAL SPEAR

CAMBRIDGE
November 1948

Note to Fourth Edition

FOR this, the fourth edition, very little change has been made in the main body of the work, and the last chapter of conclusions has been left untouched. But Chapter XIII of the last Home University Library Edition, entitled 'The First Years of Independence', and covering both India and Pakistan, clearly needed revision. It has been replaced by two chapters dealing with each country separately. The first of these covers Indian affairs during Jawaharlal Nehru's premiership until his death; the second Pakistani affairs to the re-election of President Ayub Khan a few months later. Both the death of Nehru and the re-election of Ayub marked the end of one period and the beginning of another in the development of their respective countries. The time for a considered historical judgement on the critical and formative years of the sub-continent since 1947 has clearly not yet come, but neither could such a period be left without some comment. Finally, a new bibliography for these two chapters has been added.

T.G.P.S.

India, Pakistan, and the West

1
Problems

INDIA HAS BEEN TRADITIONALLY REGARDED as a land of wonder and mystery, a place where strange people live and strange things happen. This tradition was established by the Greeks, whose first observer of whom we have any record embellished his account of India in the sixth century B.C. with marvels. The Skiapodes, he said, were a race with feet so large, that they were able to use them as sunshades, while others had ears of equal proportions in which they could wrap themselves against the cold. Herodotus followed with the story of ants 'larger than foxes but smaller than dogs' who threw out gold dust from their diggings in the desert, which was then procured by ingenious and hazardous means. From this it was but a step to the story told by Ctesias of a creature like a lion with a human face, shooting stings from its tail, and that of Megasthenes concerning a race 'of gentler manners', who had no mouths. They lived on the fumes of roast meat and the·scent of fruits and flowers, but suffered severely from the odours of cities because of their unusually sensitive nostrils. These stories were incorporated by Herodotus, Strabo, and others in their works, became part of the classical literary tradition, and so descended to western Europe.

The European visitors to India in the sixteenth and seventeenth centuries added the elements of splendour and wealth to the existing tradition. The early Portuguese reported the magnificence of Vijayanagar in the Hindu south, and the Frenchman Bernier, who practised for nine years as a doctor (1660–69) at the Moghul court of Aurangzeb, vividly described the pomp of the Muslim rulers of the north. He compared the palace of Delhi with Versailles. The new tradition took root in England through such sources as the report of James I's ambassador to the Moghuls, Sir Thomas Roe, and Dryden's play *The Tragedy of Aurangzebe*, for which Bernier was the source. Clive and the English nabobs strengthened the tradition in the eighteenth century, and the attractive prospects offered by an Indian career continued it until recent times. The popular novel and the cinema have fed both traditions down to the present day.

Thus it comes about that for one man who thinks of India as a place of heat and dust, of physical and nervous strain, there are ten who think vaguely of marble palaces and rajah's jewels, of a land of wonder and wealth and mystery. Both pictures have their element of truth, but in fact rubies are less obvious than mosquitoes, big-game shooting than daily routine in trying circumstances, and romantic princes than mundane individuals with whom one has to deal.

But this emphasis on the abnormal has its significance. It is the reaction of the mind to the strange and the little understood. It is recognition in the popular imagination of the fact of difference. Consciousness of this difference and the inability to grasp its exact nature have provided exaggeration, distortion, and pure fantasy. Men have been ready to credit, not only marvels and riches, but also stories of incredible virtue and equally improbable vice.

More analytic minds have probed deeper and interpreted this difference in terms of conflict. There is the political conflict of nationalism, the communal conflict of Hindu and Muslim, of caste and outcaste, the racial conflict of white and brown. All these have their measure of reality, but behind them lies a conflict more difficult to define as it is more difficult to grasp and more subtle in its action, the conflict of culture and civilization, of fundamental attitudes to life. The European finds this conflict difficult to comprehend because he has little knowledge of it in his own experience; all the Western world has a common cultural heritage derived from the Greeks, Romans, and Jews, and when everything has been said about national cultures, the fact remains that they are largely local variations on common themes. In India the theme itself is different, and therein lies the root difficulty in mutual understanding for both Europeans and Indians alike. The European in considering India has not only to deal with a people of alien history, traditions, climate, and habits, but with differing modes of thought, fundamental assumptions, and standards of values. The Indian in considering the problems of his own country has not only to deal with his own past history and cultural traditions, but with a wealth of ideas which are surging in from the West. Western influence does not merely consist in material novelties like guns or machine goods, type-writers or electric fans; it is fundamentally a set of ideas about life and reality of which these are the superficial symbols. The conflict of East and West is essentially a conflict of ideas, and it will be settled not by the acceptance of any one political formula, the adoption of specific Western inventions or of some particular social system, but by a synthesis of competing ideas which will eventually find expression in a new civilization and social order. India is today a land of violent contrasts and painful tensions not because its people are strange or abnormal, but because it is at present the scene of an acute conflict of fundamental ideas. The struggles and tensions of the West today are severe, but they are conflicts about the application of accepted ideas in new and perplexing circumstances. In China there is conflict of the same type as in India, but it is essentially less severe because the Chinese and Western attitudes to life are much nearer each other. The same holds good for the Muslim world. He who looks on the surface of Indian affairs is liable to be baffled by the complexity of detail and the apparent incompatibility of rival interests and ideas. The superficial observer, however acute, is like a man who judges the ocean by measuring the surface wavelets of a choppy sea. It is the ground-swell which gives notice of the coming storm.

The modern traveller to India will probably arrive in Bombay by sea or in Karachi or Delhi by air. His first impression, apart from the general strangeness of any new country, is likely to be climatic. Landing at Karachi he will at first experience the glare of the sun and soon feel its heat; he will hear and perhaps feel mosquitoes, and be disturbed at night by the wailing jackals. He will soon discover the sharp changes of temperature which make the winter further north both pleasant and treacherous to the newcomer. A brief glimpse of the sandy wastes of Rajputana, its blue lakes and stark mountain outlines, will be succeeded by a sight of the mingled greens and browns of North India with its whitewashed cities and flat-roofed mud-walled villages, its irrigated green belts, its endless expanse of plain, its mango groves and spreading trees. He will be enchanted by the winter season, with its blue skies and calm weather, its moonlight and crisp night air, its occasional northern wind and wintry showers and touch of English mud, its flowers, the bright yellowing of the flowering mustard, and the fresh green of the ripening corn. If he stays into the hot weather he will find himself in a new world in the space of about four weeks. The 'vagrant winds of Hindustan' will seem to come straight from a furnace, and dust will fill the air. There will be dust in the air and across the sun, dust in the roads and fields, dust in the bungalows and offices, dust everywhere. The whirl of electric fans will become so familiar as to pass unnoticed, and he will experience a craving for ice and cold drinks, and the parched exhaustion and frayed nerves which overtake a man working day after day at temperatures of 110° F. and over. Then comes the monsoon with its first refreshing showers and storms, followed by swarms of winged insects and innumerable creeping things; its interlude, sometimes of weeks, of panting humid heat, its hopes and fears about rain and crops, and its occasional calamities of hurricanes and flood.

The traveller who lands at Bombay or Calcutta will find himself at once in the general type of conditions associated with the tropical east. The characteristic is the palm in all its varieties, the typical scene of brilliant green. There are hills, but not too high; there is heat, but not to excess except for short periods; the climate is more of a piece and varies not so much between heat and cold as between wet and dry. In the coast towns he will learn to look for the sea breeze to freshen the stifling air of mid-morning and to take for granted the constant use of cotton clothes and a permanent feeling of dampness. Above all, he will be struck by the perpetually humid air, the unwisdom of needless physical exertion, and the necessity of taking exercise in strictly limited quantity. There is beauty in the tropical east and south, but it is a beauty to be enjoyed passively rather than actively.

Wherever the traveller may land in India he is likely to find his way before long to 'the hills'. Whether they be the moderate hills of Assam or South India or the great Himalayan range itself, the first visit is likely to make an abiding impression. The sudden change from heat to coolness, from plain to mountain, the complete new world which opens out, sharpens the mind, stimulates the imagination, and freshens the spirit. In the south and east, rolling downlands will stir nostalgic memories; in the north, hill towns clinging to knife-edge ridges dropping precipitously to ravines thousands of feet below, vistas of the great snowy range, stately forests of pine and cedar and deodar, will add a touch of awe to the jaded palate of modern experience. Whoever has seen the morning light on Kinchinjunga, or the sunset glow on the Tibetan mountains, or the full moon rising on range upon range, has added something unforgettable to his experience.

Returning to more mundane matters, an impression which is sure to grave itself upon the newcomer's mind is that of noise. There is the noise of travelling. The long journeys involve night travel, and the confused clamour of an Indian station is something unique of its kind, which is commonly first taken for a riot. But the apparent din of conflict is due only to third-class passengers adjusting themselves or porters bustling with the luggage, and later the medley is particularized into the chants of the tea-man, water-boy, and sweet-seller, the staccato commands of the staff, the entreaties of those having seats without tickets and those having tickets without seats. The noise of the city bazaar is also *sui generis* and quite unlike the dull roar of a Western city; here again, particular sounds like the musical cries of street vendors, the litanies of Muslim shopkeepers in the early morning, the Muezzin's stately call to prayer, or the hurried wailing of a Hindu funeral, once heard are never forgotten.

These external impressions, along with tourist glimpses of mosques and temples, palaces and gardens, must, like all first impressions, give place to others; impressions of obvious things are followed by those of obvious people. Every one knows the medley of costumes and types which throngs an Indian street. At first the newcomer will have the curious feeling that all faces are alike and that only the clothes are different; gradually there follows the realization that features and complexions vary as much as they do in one's own part of the world, if not more, and that there is in addition a much greater variety of costume and deportment. Picturesqueness has not yet departed from the Indian street or office or government residence. Many a newcomer has mistaken the scarlet-robed government messenger with turban and ceremonial dagger for a prince or high-born chief. European dress has not spoilt the variety, but added one more (and less graceful) item to the collection. Soon one learns to distinguish groups and races and even religions, for dress varies with community. From individuals one proceeds to groups and group actions. The peasant cultivator, the shopkeeper or ubiquitous *bania*, the patient clerk, the humble casual labourer and his sturdy womenfolk with their ample swaying skirts, graceful carriage, and head-borne burdens, all stand out in turn. Then come social events like the congregational Friday prayers at the great mosques in the big cities, or the mass devotions in spontaneously ordered lines on Muslim feast-days, or Hindu processions and mass performances of epic dramas, the festival of lights when the cities twinkle with thousands of earthenware lamps, and the great religious fairs on the banks of the sacred rivers.

All these impressions are lost on the traveller if he thinks of them merely as a gorgeous scene or a fascinating show. They lead on naturally to the lives and thoughts and problems of the people. The Indian people look and behave differently because they think and feel differently. It is easy to assume that those who are different must be wrong or peculiar, and it is the first axiom in the understanding of India that things may be different and that people may think and act otherwise than ourselves without thereby being labelled as wrong or perverse or odd. There is a reason for these differences, and the value of these first impressions consists in stimulating the mind to probe beneath the surface of Indian life and so to penetrate to the secret of the Indian problem.

Visitors to India during the World Wars were often astonished to find large numbers of Indians who spoke English, wore European clothes, and followed European habits. Alternatively, they were surprised that although wearing European clothes and speaking English they were not also English in thought, mind, and spirit. But this large class, from the official and the polished gentleman who speaks English better than we do, to the booking-clerk and the southern taxi-driver whose English is far otherwise, is the natural bridge across which the stranger must seek contact with the Indian mind. In one sense they are not the best bridge across which to reach the heart of India for they are the one class who have been most obviously influenced and modified by Western influences. Whether appreciative or critical of these things (and most Indians are both), their very consciousness of them induces a self-consciousness about their own culture which makes for selection, suppression, or over-emphasis, and so forms a barrier to unbiased comprehension. But unless one is prepared to build one's own bridge by learning an Indian language (which would then only admit you to one part of India) they are the only bridge available. Let us therefore hasten across without worrying too much about its architecture.

Once across the bridge we find ourselves in a land of problems. It is a commonplace to say that all ages are ages of transition, but in India the sense of transition and of pressing problems is specially strong in contrast to the tradition of the unchanging East. The newcomer, fresh from a Western world in ferment and doubt, and hoping here to find wisdom and stability, is shocked to discover that world itself in dissolution and anxiously asking the familiar questions: whence have we come, whither are we going, why and wherefore? The first problem that strikes him is politics. A century ago the first reaction of his Indian friends would have been curiosity not unmixed with pity. Fifty years ago it would have been philosophical or theological, the pity turned to interest with a touch perhaps of admiration; even thirty years ago a man might be asked as the first question of the first Indian who spoke to him on his first journey from Bombay: Do you believe in Destiny? But today the chances are over-whelming that the first serious conversation will concern politics. Politics is the King Charles's head of Indian social intercourse. Until recent years the subject was mainly speculative: the sins of Government, the appropri-ate line of political progress, and the shortcomings of the British.

Constitutional advance was the absorbing topic. As independence approached, the discussion assumed a more realistic tone. It concerned itself with the steps necessary to obtain independence and the desirability or otherwise of Partition. Independence was the central theme and the undertone was thoughts of power. For many years the discussions were in terms of concessions; the political leaders were in the position of agitators hoping for concessions from an all-powerful government in preference, perhaps, to this or that concession to another leader. Then they were in terms of power, growing more bitter among Indians themselves as the prospect of the final transfer of power by the British increased. Now they concern the relations of the two states and all the problems which independence has brought to each.

The political problem is a real one, but it does not concern what was British India alone. There is the further problem of the place of the old princely class in the new India, and the question (imperfectly appreciated as yet by most people) of the place of India and Pakistan as independent states in the modern world, and their relations with their neighbours and the Great Powers. Connected with the political problems are all sorts of administrative questions such as recruitment to the Services and local administration. They may be comprehended in the question, how can India and Pakistan, with their limited resources, build up and maintain a full-scale modern administration?

But it would be a grave mistake to suppose that because politics is the most discussed problem in India it is the only or even the main one. One cannot go far in social intercourse, travel, or personal observation without perceiving that there are others whose true proportions will be grasped more fully as the political question becomes less absorbing. The first of these is the poverty of India. A walk down a Calcutta street or a Delhi bazaar or a village lane is enough to compel its recognition as a grim reality. Every Indian crowd affords living and convincing testimony of this fact. As in the days of Haroun al Raschid of Baghdad, the beggar sits at the door of the palace and the hungry cry for bread. The huts, officially described as 'coolie lines', which spring up wherever constructional work is proceeding, show what custom considers fit for the labourer, and the model clerks' quarter in the capital demonstrates the higher standards of the middle classes. The crowds on station platforms, the mendicants with quavering voices who stand between the rails below higher-class carriages, the poor physique of numbers, all tell the same story. Poverty in India is a great and abiding fact, whatever its cause, duration, or possibility of cure. India may not be poorer as a whole than she was in the days of

Queen Elizabeth and the Emperor Akbar, but relatively to the West, with its new-found mechanical means of wealth, she was becoming steadily poorer. And since the small industrial class is able to multiply its wealth just as its models can do in the West (because it uses the same means) the gulf between the very rich and very poor is steadily widening. There is a greater gulf in all-round squalor and misery between the Bombay or Ahmedabad mill-owner today and his mill-worker than between an average old-time Rajah and his peasant cultivator.

Allied to poverty is the question of health. No one can be long in India without realizing that there is something seriously wrong with its health as a whole. In big and small cities, it is true, will be found modern and well-equipped hospitals; there are many dispensaries; there are medical officers who make recommendations to the local bodies. There are said to be as many Western-trained doctors per head in the big cities as in some countries in Europe and some of them are very good indeed. Yet a little observation will convince anyone that not all is healthy in the state of India. The frequent absences of most classes of workers, from fevers of various kinds, contrasts with the comparative regularity of the Western worker; the frequent epidemics from malaria to cholera and plague; the high death rate and infant mortality; the lethargic movements and lack-lustre attitudes of many, and the early onset of old age, all point to a low standard of health compared with current standards in the West. In public health it is the same. There are filtered water supplies in the towns, there are corps of vaccinators and plenty of people to say what ought to be done. But many public drains are still open, sanitation, even in large cities, is often rudimentary, social cleanliness as distinct from ceremonial and personal is still far off from godliness. The idea that prevention is better than cure is by no means generally obvious to a society which lacks the scientific outlook and so also a belief in the efficacy of the human will allied to reason and a knowledge of natural cause and effect. The visitor to a village will find that the spraying of wells to kill mosquito larvae is regarded as a peculiar talisman against fever rather than a manipulation of natural forces in favour of man. The observer in cities will still find pious people who think it a religious duty to release rats from cages in a plague-infected town, or to feed ants with sugar, rather than to cleanse bazaars and markets. A sign of the public attitude is the opposition which is apt to appear in local bodies when suggestions are made for health measures which would cost money in terms of the local rates.

A healthy India could, by a judicious application of its energy, become a wealthy India; a wealthy India could purchase the instruments of health; once set in motion in either direction the wheel would revolve to prosperity. But how many Indians? How many people can the country maintain? And has the limit been reached? A first impression reveals in the cities crowds of apparently idle people in the streets (it did so even in wartime); contact could not go far even before the war without revealing extensive middle-class unemployment and severe pressure on available occupations. But these impressions were not in themselves conclusive and might be put down to local or passing conditions. Only slowly, by noting the large families everywhere prevalent and the anxiety to provide for sons and now also for daughters, by observing the small and diminishing peasant holdings in the country, the pressure on the cultivable land, and the steady encroachment of cultivation on the intermediate land of uncertain rainfall, by studying statistics and noting the phenomenal growth of population since 1872, and by grasping the process which has turned India, during the last generation, from a grain-exporting to a grain-importing country, will the existence of a population problem force itself upon the mind. But once implanted there it will loom large indeed. India has not only to make her people healthy and wealthy, she has also to make them wise in the matter of numbers. The Indian population nearly doubled in the last seventy years, and in the last recorded decade increased by more than the population of Great Britain.

A problem which is much more easily grasped, because it is widely visible and everywhere talked about, is that of industrial development. Fifty years ago it might have been largely overlooked or dismissed as so many local manifestations of Western enterprise not typical of the country, in such places as Calcutta, Kanpur, and Bombay. But today India stands eighth in the list of the world's industrial nations; she has the largest single iron and steel works in the world. Old industries like cotton-spinning and new ones like iron-smelting, sugar-refining, and aluminium manufacture are substantially in Indian hands. There is a body of industrialists who wield great influence in the country and Indian leaders as a whole have become machine-conscious. They have become aware that India has far larger resources than those yet tapped, and they look to the development of those resources to raise the Indian standard of life and to place India on a level with the Great Powers of the world. The Bombay Plan of 1943 was their profession of faith and hope and its general acceptance in principle by Indian opinion is a measure of the forward-looking spirit of modern India.

But problems are not limited to the physical and material. If they were they would be comparatively simple for all the largeness of their scale, and

a new India might be hammered out in a few years by a group of determined men, as Ataturk and his friends wrought a new Turkey after the
first World War. While everyone wants a brave new India, there is little
agreement as to what kind of new India would be brave. Both India and
Pakistan are crying for the light, but are uncertain as to the shade of light;
they are determined to build for themselves their own national temple,
but are undecided as to the towers and terraces which shall adorn it. Shall
it be a Hindu temple, a Muslim mosque, a combination of the two, an
English mansion, an American skyscraper, or a streamlined Western
factory? Now that self-determination has been achieved it is clear that it
cannot be all these at once. 'There can be no progress in one direction
without giving things up in another,' and it is only when one achieves the
power of getting the things one wants that one realizes that something
else will have to be given up in exchange. For the Indian mind is not a
tabula rasa as one may imagine that of primitive peoples to be, who turn
their backs on their past and embrace whole-heartedly Western civilization as something greater and grander than anything they have known
before. On the contrary, it is full of traditional values and ideas which are
the fruits of prolonged meditation and age-old experience, ideas which are
rooted in reason as well as custom, which are the expression of syntheses
slowly and painfully developed and not to be cast aside like faded fashions
in a day or a year. So arise the tensions of the mind which constitute
the greatest of all the problems of India. It is the cultural problems, the
great *quo vadis?* of the Indian spirit. Signs of such tension meet the
observer at every turn. The embarrassment of the Western-returned
Indian who finds that his relations expect from him not new ideas of how
to live, but improved means of livelihood; the vacillations between
Eastern and Western schools of medicine when death overshadows a
loved relation, resulting often in a resort to several doctors of both schools
at once to the general frustration of all; the anguish often caused by the
clash of Western ideals of conduct with traditional social rules and
restrictions, are examples in the sphere of personal relations. In social
matters the same forces are at work. There are many cases where modern
scientific theories conflict, not only with custom or sentiment, but also
with accepted principles based on philosophical presuppositions. Shall
animate life be destroyed, for example, to improve stock or save suffering,
although all life is sacred? Mr. Gandhi felt that dilemma acutely when he
ordered the killing of a sick calf on his settlement at Wardha because it
was in pain, and found that he had shocked Hindu orthodoxy. Humani-
tarian work, such as inoculation and measures for preventing disease,

encounters Hindu objections of touch or dirt or ceremonial cleanliness. Agricultural reform encounters religious objections to the killing and the scientific breeding of stock and is opposed to the whole Hindu and Muslim systems of inheritance and land division, and various systems of joint ownership and enterprise. How is the debt problem to be solved when a main motive for incurring debts among the thrifty Hindus is a religious or semi-religious one, the proper performance of family ceremonies by which a man's status in society is determined? The task of raising the standard of the public services is faced with the tradition of family loyalty, which regards duty to the family as paramount to duty to the State. All democratic processes and measures are dogged by the subtly pervasive spirit of hierarchy and class which pervades Indian society. Orthodox Hinduism can see all men as brothers perhaps in the whole of time taken together, but not at any given moment, for all men have lived before and most will live again, and their position today is the sum-total of their yesterdays. Or, if they are still brothers, they are unequal brothers with unequal duties. No man is born free in the Hindu system; he seeks freedom and hopes to obtain it generations hence. Thus the eager millenarianism of the Western materialist is damped by doubt and cynicism. There is no one more religious than the Hindu and no one more sceptical. It is this variation of value which makes so many observers regard the Indian world as topsy-turvy, a looking-glass world where everything goes by opposites. In reality it has its own rules which are different from those of Europe. Apply democratic principles to India and the results are surprising, because the Hindu doctrine of man is different from the European concept; apply Western science and the results are surprising again, because the Hindu theory of nature and the world is quite other than the European; apply philanthropic notions and the results vary once more, because the Hindu idea of man and his duty is different from that of the West.

Having admitted all this, it must not be supposed that the whole Western influence in India is a mere veneer or that it is only a matter of modern conveniences and instruments of power. It has penetrated the Indian soil, though no one knows how deeply. It is changing the Indian outlook, though no one knows how radically. It is fermenting in the Indian mind, though no one can say with what final result. Whether the two sets of values can live side by side indefinitely, whether one must oust the other and what the consequence of this would be, whether there can be a borrowing without radical transformation as Ram Mohan Roy hoped, or a synthesis of the two as Tagore believed, is the problem of problems facing India today. It is the problem to which all other questions, racial, social, political, scientific, or religious, however large they may loom in themselves, are related, and of which they are aspects.

2
The Country

INDIA IS SO VAST and its conditions so varied, and it is so easy to judge the whole by a report of a part, that some description of the country as a whole is necessary for an understanding of the Indian problem. India is a sub-continent in the sense that it forms a geographical whole and is physically cut off from the rest of Asia except in the north-west; and even there access has not been easy and intercourse only occasional. As far as the rest of Asia is concerned it might have been a separate continent altogether; India has given Asia far more than it has borrowed, and its development has been fundamentally its own. For this reason contrasts of Asia with Europe and loose talk of East and West are out of place. When you speak of Asia, which part of Asia have you in mind? When you enlarge upon 'the East', of what kind of East are you thinking? Indian civilization and Indian people differ quite as much from Chinese as they do from European, and the Muslim Middle East with its Semitic background is again a different world. South-east Asia has a cultural affinity with India and China, it is true, but this is because both cultures have spread and met there, producing something akin to both, but identical with neither. South-east Asian culture is the result of Sino-Indic cultural imperialism without any evidence of common Eastern or Asiatic features. Looking north one comes to the Mongolian world, peopled today by tribes secluded and quiescent, but once the terror impartially of India, China, and Europe.

The boundaries of the Indian sub-continent, apart from the sea and the Himalayas and the Hindu Kush in the north, extend through Afghanistan and Baluchistan to the west, and a tangle of hill and jungle and swamp on the east and north-east. The most effective of all barriers in the east has been rain with its sister fever, so that intercourse between

China and India has actually proceeded through Central Asia and the north-west or by sea through Indonesia rather than over the mountains of Shensi or the Assamese hills. Only by sea or through the north-western passes has there been any serious contact with the outside world, either in the past or today. Even the north-western passes did not give any easy access to the country. Those which debouch on Sind lead on to an obstacle more serious than mountain or forest, the waterless western half of the Rajputana desert. It is only the Khyber and its neighbours which lead through the Punjab corridor to the northern Indian plain.

In shape India may be described as a triangle with its apex pointing downwards, with a shallow rectangle imposed on its base and overlapping to the west, and a square box placed on the overlapping portion of the rectangle. The triangle is peninsular India, the rectangle the northern Indian plain, Rajputana, Gujarat, and Sind, and the box Kashmir and the northern Punjab. Geographically it may be divided into four main portions and a number of subsidiaries. First comes the north-western mountain area, a wheel with a hollow centre, which is the vale of Kashmir. Apart from the annual tourist traffic, this region before Partition was secluded; the belief which is still cherished there that Kashmir is the centre of the world, forms one of the major hurdles in the process of enlightening its youth; Kashmiris, like Cornishmen crossing the Tamar, still look upon a journey to the plains as going abroad. The second region is the great northern Indian plain, which stretches from the Kashmir foot-hills and the hills of the Salt Range to the Bay of Bengal. It runs roughly from north-west to south-east and is bounded on the south first by the encroaching Rajputana desert and then by the jungles and hills of Central India. Delhi is 900 miles from Calcutta and 600 feet above sea-level, and the watershed between the Jumna and the Sutlej is so slight as to be invisible to the naked eye. Most of this plain is very fertile and its cultivation depends upon the limits of rainfall and the possibilities of irrigation. The third region is the Rajputana desert, which fills the space between the northern plain and Sind, and its extension across Sind to Baluchistan. The main characteristic of this region is lack of rain in varying degrees. Its aridity has kept it poor; its inaccessibility has kept it free and made it a region of refuge, with the result that it has become a museum of Indian history, a citadel of romantic tradition and the picturesque. The last region covers the peninsula from the river Narbada to Cape Comorin. The coastal fringe is a low-lying, rice-growing tropical belt, while the interior is a tableland sloping gradually from west to east, and shading off in the north into the valleys of the Tapti and the Narbada, and the forests and broken country which separate the Deccan (or south land) from the northern plain. In the extreme south are blocks of hills rising to 8,000 feet which provide sanatoria for Europeans and Indians alike, retreats for the elderly, and estates on their slopes for the tea and coffee planters.

Connected with the four main regions are a number of subsidiary areas, and it is worth mentioning some of these. Flanking the Indus to the north-west lies the frontier country, a region of arid stony hills, of extremes of climate, and of turbulent frontier tribes. Its strategical importance and the character of its inhabitants place it apart from the rest of India and compel special mention. Then comes the province of Sind, which comprises the lower course of the Indus and its delta. It is a land like Egypt, but without its monuments. It is a rainless area whose riverine culture depends entirely upon irrigation. Perhaps one of the primary cradles of civilization, it has stood apart both from the rest of India and from the Middle East, being bounded on all sides by deserts and inhospitable mountains. Crossing the marshes of Cutch one comes to the fertile province of Gujarat, shut in between the desert to the north and the sea. Its produce and its seaboard led to a maritime trade with the Middle East, and its ports of Cambay and Surat were for centuries the outlets for the products of northern India, and the gateways for Western commerce until eclipsed by Bombay with its ocean traffic. Through these ports, also, passed the famous pilgrim traffic to Mecca. At the eastern end of the great plain lies Bengal, a land of rivers and rain and rice, whose wealth has always tempted invaders and whose climate has usually enervated them. East again lies Assam, a temperate hilly region, whose down-like hills encouraged tea planting and the European settler.

Moving south towards the Deccan we reach the large region of forest and hill and uncertain rainfall whose eastern half is known historically as Gondwana and in the mass as Central India. Its lack of resources and, still more, its lack of communications has kept it apart from the main stream of Indian life and made it the most effective historical barrier to the unification of India. In the south there are two areas which call for special mention. The first is Malabar, the coastal strip running south from just north of Cannanore to Travancore. Cut off from the hinterland by jungles and hills, it has looked to the sea, and its possession of spices has made it an entrepôt of traffic between East and West. The Romans visited it regularly from the time of the discovery of the monsoon early in the first century A.D. and, after them, the Arabs. Chinese junks called regularly as late as the fifteenth century, while Malabar ships traded with Africa and Arabia on the one side and Indonesia on the other. It was here that Vasco da Gama, in 1497, arrived on the first through voyage from Europe. Travancore is geographically a part of Malabar, but it has a larger coastal plain and is distinguished by a continuous history from pre-Christian times. This region by its isolation has become a museum of sociological survivals, and it is also notable for the existence of a substantial Christian community from at least the sixth century. Last must be mentioned the great Himalayas themselves, which embrace all the climates—from the tropical jungles of the foothills to the arctic wastes of the great snowy range. The inhabitants are few and the struggle for existence severe; before the vogue for hill stations and sanatoria, few visited them without compulsion. But the mountains have always bulked large in Indian imagination. Here are the resorts of Siva and the high gods of the Hindu pantheon and the retreats of the *rishis* or sages; here pilgrims still march painfully to ice-bound caves and holy springs, and ascetics seek union with the One. The Himalayas overshadow all Indian thought as they dominate and bound the Indian sub-continent.

The rivers of India are mighty and intimately connected with Indian life. But outside Bengal, where they still hold their own against railways as means of communication, they are important more for what they are than for what they carry. Until British times the Ganges and the Jumna were exceptions, being arteries of commerce from Delhi to Bengal, but now they too have been largely displaced, first by the Grand Trunk Road and then by the railway. In the utilitarian sense they have been throughout history almost useless until the British, in the nineteenth century, put them to work in a series of vast irrigation schemes.[1] They have not been barriers because they are seasonal and are fordable for many months of the year. Their role in Indian life has been that of objects of worship and places of resort. In the rivers (if one can be found) the devout Hindu bathes at dawn and performs his devotions; on their banks his funeral pyre is built and burnt, and over their waters his ashes are scattered. On their banks temples are built, for water plays an essential part in Hindu worship, and to holy spots beside the more sacred rivers pilgrims resort for fairs and festivals. It is no accident that Kashi or Benares, the most sacred city of all, is on the Ganges, or that Mathura, the birthplace of the god Krishna, stands on the Jumna. Pilgrimage to holy places on river sites is the Hindu form of vacation. In the West one sails

[1] The canals of Firoz Shah and the Moghuls are the honourable exceptions which prove the rule.

on a river; in China one admires it and sometimes drowns in it; in India one worships it.

The commonest of mistakes about India is to suppose that its climate is uniform and that it is always hot. Enough has already been said to indicate the fallacy of this view, and it only remains to distinguish the four main varieties of climate. There is first the cold climate of the northern Alpine regions. These all experience severe winters and cool summers, the climatic scheme being diversified east of Kashmir by heavy monsoon rains in the summer months. A curious feature is the unusual height of the sun for the coolness of the climate, while the rarefied air produces the effect so pronounced in Tibet and the Andes—of great heat in the direct rays of the sun together with great cold in the immediately adjacent shade. Another feature is the variety of climate in the hills themselves, caused by the height of the hillsides. An hour's scramble from any hill station will lead to another climate, and a few hours' march from Narkunda, in the Simla hills, passes through all the varieties from Alpine to tropical.

The second type is continental, covering the northern Indian plain from the frontier to the borders of Bengal. There is a marked cold weather with temperatures falling sometimes to freezing-point, and, in the Punjab, below it. In Moghul and early British times ice was regularly manufactured during cold spells, stored in pits, and used when the hot weather came on. During this season all the flowers of the temperate zone will grow in profusion wherever water is to be found. The hot dry season follows, with temperatures rising up to 120° F. More exhausting than the heat by day are the breathless heavy nights, when the thermometer refuses to fall below 90° F.; and most exhausting of all is the dust which hangs like an iron pall over the sky for days together, obscuring the sun and cloaking the moon, periodically precipitating itself in short, sharp storms. This period is, however, healthy because the heat and the desiccation banish insects. The monsoon follows; copious in the east, but scanty and capricious to the west. The relief of cooler air is followed by days of stifling humidity; mosquitoes breed and fever takes its toll. As the monsoon dries off, these fevers reach their height, until in October or November the real cold weather sets in. In the desert regions the type of climate is essentially the same, but the contrasts of temperature between day and night and summer and winter are greater.

The third climatic type is, of course, the tropical, which for many means India. The tropical type proper prevails along the east and west coasts and in Bengal, though even in Bengal there is a brief cold weather which provides an excuse for lighting fires. Profuse vegetation and waving palm-trees, damp heat, slight differences of temperature, and an exuberant insect life are all there, and variations of rainfall rather than of heat and cold mark the seasons. The forests are forests and not merely waste places covered with scrub, crops can be raised twice a year, and one experiences the characteristically tropical feeling of lassitude.

In the Deccan or peninsular plateau and across the belt of central Indian hills and jungles there is a type associated with the tropical regions, but not entirely of it. Lack of rainfall and moderate elevation of the land, a drier and less enervating air, tend to modify the tropical features without replacing them by the temperate balance of heat and cold. Indians, no less than Europeans, are often deceived by the fallacious supposition of a single Indian climate, and it is not uncommon to see shivering people from the south, arrived in the north to attend Christmas conferences, clad only in cotton garments, seeking for blankets and mufflers.

Lack of good communications has been one of the main economic and political difficulties of India through the ages. As has been said earlier, the rivers, except the Ganges, the Jumna, and the Bengal waterways, afforded little help, and the only alternatives were tracks for carts and mules and camels. If the climate did not, as in England, forbid all movement in the winter by turning the roads into seas of mud, floods impeded movement during the monsoon and the mere fact of distance and the lack of carrying capacity made for isolation. It took three months to travel from Delhi to Bengal and more from Delhi to the south. Until a hundred years ago famine in one province could not be relieved from the surplus of another, through the physical impossibility of moving goods in bulk quickly enough. Two-thirds of the population of the Delhi district died in the great famine of 1782 on account of a shortage which was essentially local. Luxury goods of small bulk and great profit could be moved far and wide, but the various regions lived their basic lives to themselves. Strong governments arranged systems of posts with relays of horses, and the Moghuls maintained in the north a trunk road whose stately milestones can still be seen, but these served mainly for official communications or military movement. Until modern times India's communications were rather as those of Europe would be if all communications were cut off except by air. Only the rich or ascetics could travel far and none could carry much.

Today India has a network of both roads and railways. The roads were started first on the Moghul pattern and with the Romans in mind, but it is upon the railways that India really depends. All heavy goods, except for a small coastal traffic, must go by rail, which means that the supply of the great cities, the distribution of industrial products, the moving of raw materials, and the transport of grain all depend upon one form of transport. When the maintenance and supply of a modern army were added to these tasks in the war the railways were grievously strained. The industrialization of India must strain them further, for there is no alternative long-distance mode of transport in sight. Motors require petrol, and since there is little oil in India it is the railways that must carry the spirit inland.

It remains to ask how far the geography of India has promoted its internal unity. It has not, as in Europe, tended to separate its peoples into well-defined areas and so to promote the growth of separate national entities. But neither has it thrown them together in a bowl, as in the Middle West of America, and so produced a uniform type from a medley of differing constituents. Geography has promoted partial and hindered complete unity. It has encouraged aspirations to empire and hindered its maintenance. The geographical factor has been working all through Indian history and is active even today, despite roads and railways. From the north-western passes and the Attock crossing of the Indus a funnel between the Salt Range and the Kashmir hills leads into the Punjab corridor, flanked by the Himalayas and the desert, and this in turn, without any perceptible natural obstacle, opens into the great Gangetic plain, down which one can proceed to the sea without seeing a hill. Along the line of the Jumna and in the region of Delhi a road turns south; it follows the plain as far as the Chambal and meets no serious obstacle until it reaches the great Narbada river and the Vindhyan range of mountains. This northern half of India forms a strategical whole which can be most conveniently dominated by a strong power along the line of the Jumna. Access to all parts of the region is easy except to Rajputana, on account of its desert condition, and even there accessible Ajmir provided a centre for general strategical dominance, though not for detailed tactical control. This region is the historical Hindustan and the seat of successive empires throughout Indian history.

Between Hindustan and the Deccan or south country lies the jungle and hill tangle of Central India. The hills are not very lofty and the jungles not specially tangled, but the combination of size with sparsely peopled and wild tracts has afforded a most effective obstacle to large-scale contact between north and south. Aboriginal hill-tribes in the past, not fierce and bold like the frontiersmen, but persistent and incalculable, formed an additional danger. The reality of this jungle bar is attested by the fact that not until 1928 was Delhi directly linked by rail with Madras. This belt extends right across India from Orissa to the western *ghats*, and much of the eastern portion retained practical independence almost till British times.

The south, with its central plateau and eastern coastal plain, forms a second geographical unity which has frequently found political expression in southern empires. The significant fact about the central forest belt as an obstacle was that it was *not too difficult*. Access from either direction was possible, though, the north being stronger and richer, the movement was usually from north to south. It was possible to get across and even to take large armies across, but it was not easy to stay there or maintain garrisons for long. The political consequence of this has been that northern empires have frequently broken down in the effort to control the south, and the social consequence a marked distinction between the northern and southern Indian peoples, the most marked, perhaps, of all those which differentiate the various groups. Everything in the south differs from the north, from race and language to schools of music.

This then is a brief description of geographical India. It is a region marked by Nature as separate from the rest of the world, but also an area so divided that he who controls a part believes he can take the whole, but, stretching out his hand, finds it beyond his strength. The Moghuls broke the southern kingdoms, but the south broke the Moghuls. Though India has been the seat of a single culture, however diversely expressed, this culture has neither articulated itself in a number of independent national states as in Europe, nor as a single stable cultural empire as in China. There has been a constant striving for unity without the power of achieving it, and when at last the Sisyphean stone of unity was actually pushed to the top of the hill nearly a hundred and fifty years ago it was by an alien people using strange instruments of power. This constant see-saw between hope and disappointment, between empire and confusion, has made of Indian history a series of alternations between creative achievement and frustration.

3
The Peoples of India

THE BURLY PUNJABI, the wiry Maratha, the artistic Bengali, the saffron-marked intellectual southern Brahmin, the plausible shopkeepers, all typify India to different people according to their experience of the country; but in actual fact no one of them would be accepted by the others for a moment as the typical Indian. There is no single typical figure like John Bull or Uncle Sam, acceptable to all; apart from any question of appearance it would be difficult to agree on a name. Any Hindu figure would certainly be unacceptable to the Muslims, and no Muslim character would suit the Hindus. The typical pictorial representation of India is a woman, but she is recognizable only by the *sari* or flowing dress affected by the educated class of modern India. The reason for this is simple: there is no typical figure. Britain, with racial origins as diverse, has fused them all into a single people. America, with a similar racial medley, is doing the same. But in India the different invasions can be identified by the racial types they introduced, and often peculiar customs which they still retain. Near Taxila descendants of the Huns who burnt the city in the fifth century can still be found living under the same name.

The explanation of the distinctive racial types which persist in India is fourfold. There is first the racial factor. Scientifically speaking, India has been occupied by three main racial types—the dark-skinned Dravidians, the fair Caucasians, and the yellow-skinned Mongolians. These people have intermixed to form, along with the invaders from the North-West of the historical period, the seven main racial types of India. The next factor is that of caste. The separate racial elements set up taboos against each other which kept them substantially apart. Gradually Hindu culture prevailed over all except the forest tribes, some of which still remain untouched and the Brahmins achieved the wonderful feat of

21

convincing those below them that they ought to be inferior because of their sins in previous lives. Thus caste, with its regimentation of society into marriage groups based both on occupation and race, tended to keep the races apart, and by the device of the affiliated caste was able to fit each newly absorbed primitive tribe or each new immigrant horde into the general Hindu system. The third factor has been invasion. The coming of the Aryans is the first historical example of this, though it is likely that the Dravidians came before them, and no one yet knows exactly who were the inhabitants of Mohenjo-Daro in Sind and whence they came. From historic times there has been a series of such invasions and each has left its mark, whether in racial admixture as in Bengal, or in new caste groups as in the North West, in new communities altogether as with the Muslims in general, or in new tribal units as with the Rohillas.

Lastly, there is the geographical factor. There is first the simple fact of distance, which, during the long intervals between migrations and race movements, tended to keep groups in one place through the sheer difficulty of moving far away. Traditional Indian economics being subsistence economics, there were no very strong motives for mass movements in any direction. Famine migrations there have been, but they have been sporadic and unsystematic for the simple reason that until the last century famine might occur anywhere. The starving Gujarati might one year migrate to a prosperous northern plain only to find himself starving the next year when the crops in Gujarat were plentiful. Universal plenty and universal shortage are both gifts of the Western world to India. Besides distance, geography has helped the segregation of races in another way. We have already noted that the configuration of the country both encourages the aspiration of unity and hinders its fulfilment; similarly, in certain parts it encourages a certain degree of separation while hindering its development into isolation. Travancore and Kashmir and parts of Rajputana are perhaps the only three areas isolated from the rest of the country by nature, but there are a number of tracts which are separated without being completely cut off. Most of Rajputana and Central India is difficult of access but not inaccessible; that is why these areas have become refuges for groups threatened by stronger neighbours and have at the same time received Hindu culture and acknowledged successive imperial powers. Gujarat is sufficiently isolated to have a vigorous life of its own, but sufficiently wealthy and accessible to be certain of the attention of others. Difficulty of communication with the interior has given the western coastal strip a secluded but not hermetic character. The plateau of Mysore, with its moderate difficulty of access, has encouraged the growth of a characteristic culture. Bengal on one side lies open to the merchant and the soldier, but its climate, its rivers and rains have combined to give it an atmosphere which envelops each conqueror or adventurer in turn and a temperament which is sooner or later caught by all who stay there long. So while there may be a fundamental unity of culture and outlook in India, there is an almost infinite variety of action and people and language.

We may now turn to the pageant of India, that riot of colour and costume which is the delight of the tourist and the authors of popular travelogues. Taken in the mass, the idea of colourful India is in fact a myth. The 'gorgeous East' may describe some products, some individuals, some places, and some aspects of nature in India; applied to the country and its life as a whole it is a misnomer, and those who treat the multi-coloured turban, the ceremonial dress of a clansman, the jewels of a rajah as the most important things about the people who wear them help the mutual understanding neither of India nor of the West. Descriptions which are limited to marble palaces, temple pinnacles, and majestic mosques are equally misleading; they all tend to create a myth of an exotic fairyland, a never-never land of romance and mystery which is as far from actuality as the world of Tennyson's *Idylls of the King* was from the conditions of late fifth-century England. Descended from the work of eighteenth-century artists like the two Daniells and Zoffany, who found in India a new and lucrative field for the exploitation of the new Western taste for the romantic and picturesque, and the stories of men newly dazzled by the wealth to be won in the Indies, this school has falsified India by concentrating upon a mere fraction of its life. The Taj or Ajanta no more typify India than the Woolworth building typifies America. The noble monuments of India are there, but so are its huts and hovels. The colours of the rainbow can be seen walking the streets, but more often men themselves make the colour; nature has never surpassed itself in beauty in parts of India, but often she is never more grim; the seasons have their changing, but not always smiling faces; it is not accident that one of the great gods of India is Siva, the destroyer. The most characteristic colour of all is the one which the West has borrowed—khaki—the dusty colour. Equally misleading is the approach of the modern realist school, which sees India as an amalgam of mass disease, mass poverty, and mass misery. Cheerfulness will keep breaking in on the most gloomy external conditions, and not even the untouchables and industrial workers are so wretched as propagandists would have us believe. There is a pageant of India, but it is a motley one: its many colours include the sombre as well as the gay, its people range through the whole gamut from wisdom to ignorance and folly, from holiness to vice, from untold wealth to great poverty.

In separating the pageant into its constituents parts a preliminary question arises. Shall we make our division horizontally or vertically, by geographical or class groups? The vertical division seems obvious, but the caste system makes the horizontal division much more suitable than it would be in Europe or America. As the mandarin scholar-official was ubiquitous in China, so is the Brahmin in India—a thin layer of priestly intellect spread over the whole country. But in India the division is carried further: the military class is widely spread; the same type of merchant class is everywhere to be found; and there are outcastes or untouchables from Peshawar to Cape Comorin. These facts must be borne in mind, but it remains true on the whole that society is differentiated more obviously by race and locality and language than by caste, and that a clearer picture will be obtained by noting some of the principal racial groups and their characteristics. The social structure of Hinduism and Islam will be discussed in separate chapters.

The next division to be considered is that of language, for this plays a vital part in the life of India. Nobody can be long in north India without discovering that there are two languages, Hindi and Urdu, which both have claims to the status of a lingua franca. He will also discover that there is a hybrid called Hindustani, which, in spite of the purists, is much used in daily intercourse. He will further come upon a variety of scripts, some consisting apparently of dots and dashes, others of circles and crescents, and others again of straight lines and strokes. He will become aware of a battle of the scripts in progress, and notice meanwhile that English continues to be used as the one certain means of communication among the educated, and the European script as the one which is equally foreign to all. These differences only indicate the variety of the Indian languages, for the real position is much more complicated. Sir G. A. Grierson, in his linguistic survey of India, has listed 225 main languages and dialects. In actual fact, setting aside the highly localized languages of jungle tribes and hill districts, all these may be grouped around a few major languages and their derivatives. There is first the broad division between the Aryan languages of the north and the Dravidian tongues of the south. The Aryan languages are all related to Sanskrit, the highly developed form of one of the Indo-Aryan dialects. At one time it was thought to be the parent of all the Aryan languages, but it is now accepted as the sister of Greek and Latin, of ancient Persic and Avestic. As the invaders spread over

Northern India the tribal dialects tended to develop into local languages; one of them thus became the Sanskrit language, which, standardized in the early Hindu scriptures, became first the speech of the polite, and then a dead language for priests and scholars. Learned men can still converse in Sanskrit as Renaissance scholars talked in Latin. These local languages, known as *prakrits*, gradually developed literatures of their own. The *prakrit* prevalent in Northern India at the time of the rise of Buddhism was used by the Buddhist reformers for their sacred writings as being the tongue 'understanded of the people'. This in turn also became fixed and dead, and is now known as Pali. It is the sacred language of the Buddhists of Ceylon and Burma, and the vehicle of the Buddhist sacred canon. In the course of centuries the *prakrits* or local languages decayed and it is from their ruins that the modern languages of Northern India developed. All of them are related in greater or less degree to Sanskrit which throughout provided a standard of form and a reservoir of words. The chief are Bengali, Hindi in the northern plain as far as the Punjab and in Central India, Gujarati in Gujarat, Marathi along the hills of western India and stretching across the centre, Sindhi in Sind, and the Rajput dialects. These languages may be said to enjoy the same sort of affinity to each other as the Latin group in Europe. In the south comes the Dravidian family, again enjoying a general affinity, but each having its own well-developed literature. Telugu is noted for its sweetness, and all for their difficulty. The principal ones are Tamil, stretching south and inland from Madras, Telugu, covering the Andhra country, Malayalam in Travancore and Malabar, and Kannada on the Mysore plateau. In the extreme north the Islamic influence has been felt. The frontiersmen speak guttural Pushtu, an Iranian tongue, and Punjabi, though related to Hindi, has many foreign importations. Finally, the clash of Muslim invaders with Hindu has produced the interesting and elegant hybrid known as Urdu. As its Turkish name implies, it was first the language of the court and camp. It was the dialect developed by contact between the conquerors and Hindu labourers and officials who supplied their wants and carried on the subordinate administration. The court language was Persian, the euphonious Italian of the East, as remarkable for its simplicity as for its elegance. By a common linguistic process a Persian vocabulary was grafted on to a Hindi syntax and when bards began to use the resulting Urdu for their ballads and love songs, its future was assured. In the early eighteenth century the Moghul Emperor Mohammad Shah ordered his court poets to compose in Urdu instead of Persian, thus at once raising the language to respectability and recognizing

its progress. Urdu is now the language of northern Islam and also of
many Hindus from the Sutlej to the Ganges. Its line of demarcation
from Hindi is shadowy; all that can certainly be said is that each contains
elements of the other; that each looks in different directions for its
vocabulary (Hindi to Sanskrit and Urdu to Persian and Arabic) and so
tends to grow apart; that in their elementary form they are almost alike
and in their most developed form almost entirely different. The elementary resemblance has been exploited to form the Hindustani of everyday
speech. Persian influence remains strong in the north and is illustrated by
the fact that Sir Mohammad Iqbal, the greatest Urdu poet and a recognized literary figure, *preferred* to write in Persian.

The people of India can now be passed in brief review. The first and
most striking are the frontiersmen from the Khyber to Quetta with their
brethren the Baluchis. The frontier Pathans proper maintain a tribal
society with its accompaniments of valour, sensitive personal honour,
hospitality, intertribal wars, and the blood feud. The leading fact of their
life is poverty, that poverty which stirs a vigorous people to activity as it
dulls an enfeebled one to despair. The activity is usually unlawful and
takes the form of raiding the plains, cattle lifting, and the looting of
villages. In their relation to the plainsmen, their lack of resources, and
their vigour in idleness they can be compared to the pre- '45 Highlanders.
Thus the most tranquil period the frontier has enjoyed in this century was
the years when the building of the Khyber railway by providing good
money made raiding superfluous. The frontiersman's plain-dwelling
cousins in the Frontier province lead a settled life. But never far below the
surface lies a zeal for Islam which might at any moment turn their eyes
westward and still nearer the love of money of a poor and fearless people.

The Punjab, or land of the five rivers, has a strongly-marked character
of its own in spite of a heterogeneous population. There is the Muslim
Punjabi, a sturdy and sport-loving peasant, who forms the majority, the
Hindu Jat, an equally sturdy and reputedly slow-witted farmer, and the
Sikh, of largely the same stock, but quickened by the abandonment of
caste taboos into an active and versatile entrepreneur. The marks of the
modern Punjab were: expanding agriculture based on canal colonies and
irrigation; rising industries and swelling towns fed by hydro-electric
power; and communal tension. The prosperity brought by wheat crops
from irrigated lands produced a class of new rich who would have been at
home in the atmosphere of Victorian Birmingham. The Partition divided
the Punjab into two and migrations since have sorted out the communities,
Muslims moving to the West, Hindus and Sikhs to the East Punjab.

There has been much dislocation, but the vigour of the people brings hope for the future.

The Sikhs demand a special word, because they are the most noted people of the Punjab. It is important to remember, however, that though their strength now lies in the East Punjab, they do not constitute the whole even of that province. Their beards and turbans, their renunciation of smoking and compensatory taste for spirits, their vigour and initiative, are well known. Their enterprise has carried them all over the world and has led them in India wherever new openings have occurred or new opportunities offered. The Sikhs are a sect who have become a people, and they are the latest example in India of this phenomenon. Originating in the fifteenth century in one of the periodic attempts to find a common platform between Hinduism and Islam, they were driven by political events into opposition to the Moghul government and antagonism to the Muslims in general, a hostility fraught with fateful consequences in recent times. But though their general organization and outlook is now Hindu they retain certain features which still mark them as a peculiar people. They are a people of a book, like the Muslims, and this book contains specific doctrines; they have a common brotherhood and are organized in a Khalsa (or church) in spite of caste survivals within their ranks, and like the Muslims they eschew idolatry. In racial origin they are mainly Jat, but in their behaviour they might be taken for a different people. The transformation in Sikh racial character wrought by freedom from the inhibitions of Hindu customs is one of the curiosities of sociology.

To the south-west of the Punjab in the delta and lower courses of the Indus lies Sind. The rural Sindhi is a peasant tribesman just beginning to awake to the possibilities of irrigation from the Sukkur Barrage. The urban Hindu Sindhi was one of the most intelligent and enterprising people in the world. The Sindhi is ubiquitous throughout India and is to be found wherever Indian commercial communities exist abroad. Where money is to be made a Sindhi is to be found, and often in places where only a Sindhi could see an opportunity. The Sindhi's activity and ability has given him a position in the country out of all proportion to his numbers.

In the desert to the east dwell the Rajput clans, the chief source in India of the pageant myth. They certainly look the part, with their beards and coloured turbans, their swords, their castles, their dazzling lakes and marble palaces, their tradition of chivalry and fights for freedom. Actually they are one of the less significant people of India today. No longer acting as a citadel of freedom against a foreign foe, they have lost their *raison d'être*. Poverty and lack of resources have left them behind in the race for modern development, and lack of adaptability has hindered the exploitation of those opportunities which have presented themselves. The Rajput in the past has shown great courage and high gifts of states-manship, but today much opening for the latter has been wanting and war demands a trained intelligence and technical skill which he has not found easy to acquire. Innate conservatism, clan spirit, and reluctance to com-bine have parcelled out a great tract into a large number of jealous principalities, each of illustrious descent and straitened resources. The Rajputs possess the nearest approach in India to the medieval feudal system, and are a standing example in sociology of the results of breeding for a particular purpose.

Just south lies fertile Gujarat. It is a home of enterprising merchants, and its chief city Ahmedabad is a centre of Indian industrialism. The Gujarati is proverbial for thrusting individualism and, like the Sindhi, he is to be found wherever wealth is to be won. Mr. Gandhi came from one of the official families of the lesser states bordering Gujarat and Sardar Vallabhbhai Patel was a compatriot. For all their energy and belligerency the Gujaratis are not a warlike people. They have been much influenced by the Jain philosophy which believes in the inviolability of all life, and have consequently found the Gandhian doctrine of *ahimsa* or non-violence very congenial. But non-violence to a Gujarati does not mean a Tolstoyan non-resistance to evil; it means using non-violent means to get your own way, with the emphasis on getting your own way. This explains much in the non-violent tactics of Congress in the past and why non-violence sometimes seemed to the outsider less morally attractive than a little old-fashioned physical force. A pleasing facet of the Gujarati creed has been their respect for animal life. The animal hospital at Surat, the old Gujarati port, was one of the sights upon which generations of European travellers have enlarged. Gujarat was also for centuries the home of the mercantile Parsis, a community of Persian refugees from Muslim rule. Parsis and Gujaratis with the unorthodox Muslim followers of the Aga Khan share the financial control of Bombay. The Parsis number only about 100,000, but their part in Indian life has been so conspicuous that they demand a share of attention. Their opportunity as merchants arrived with the coming of the British. They developed the port of Bombay and built ships to rival the stout East Indiamen; later they developed the Bombay cotton industry and to-day are prominent as financiers, industrialists, and merchants. J. N. Tata, the maker of the Indian iron and steel industry and the great firm of Tatas, was a Parsi.

The Parsis carried with them to India the fire-venerating doctrine of Zoroaster to which they are still faithful, but more noticeable today is their very radical westernization. Apart from the mitre-like hats of the men and the Indian dress of the ladies there is little to distinguish the modern Parsi from the European.

Returning to the north we come to the people of the Jumna and Ganges basins who constitute the core of modern Hinduism. Here lives the tradition of the Hindu epics, for here stood the capitals of their hero kings, here are all the sites of their legendary conflicts, and here the holy cities of Mathura and Benares. From here come many of the leaders of the modern Hindus. Taken as a whole they are perhaps the least picturesque of all the Indian people, both in dress and behaviour. They unite intellect with practical ability and emotion with sober judgement. They possess one of the oldest aristocracies of the world in the *talukdars* of Oudh and the most conservative priesthood in the Brahmins of Benares. This region is the essential Hindustan, the land of the Hindus, the home of the modern Hindi tongue.

Through Bihar, the land of the Buddhist *viharas* or monasteries, the people by small degrees shade off into the Bengali race. In Bengal, Hindus and Muslims are found in almost equal numbers, but the Bengali character is so marked that it transcends communal distinctions. The Bengalis speak the same language, and wear the same dress, except in the towns. All possess the same nervous emotional temperament and exhibit the same love of art. Their customs differ, but this is not entirely a Muslim innovation, dating perhaps from the ascendancy of a Brahmin aristocracy over a Buddhist peasantry from the tenth century onwards. Bengal is the land of the *dhoti*, the flowing cotton garment tucked up in front and fastened behind, which does duty for trousers, and has the advantage in a humid climate of admitting air without revealing the person. Everywhere the Bengali goes he takes his *dhoti* with him, and it has become a familiar sight all over India. The distinguishing traits of the Bengali are imagination, intelligence, taste, sensitiveness, and clannishness. The qualities of imagination and intelligence are the two most immediately apparent; there are few human beings more winning than a group of laughing Bengali youths, or more attractive than a cultured Bengali lady. It is these two qualities which put the Bengali in the van of westernization. The quality of taste united to those of imagination and intelligence has produced Bengali art. They have given birth to the Bengali school of painting, modern Bengali music, and Bengali literature with Tagore at its head. The quick-witted Bengali mind has been alert to see possibilities of combining Eastern and Western technique, while an emotional heart has lingered lovingly round the heritage of India. Equally marked is the quality of sensitiveness which, like the *dhoti*, accompanies the Bengali wherever he goes. It produces moods of alternate elation and depression, an elation which sometimes turns to *hubris* in prosperity and despair in difficulty. It has, perhaps, been responsible for making the question of personal relations between the races a serious factor in Indian politics. The final quality is clannishness. It has been said that where two or three tribesmen are gathered together you have a blood feud; where two or three Muslims a feast, two or three *banias* a bazaar, and two or three Gujaratis a stock exchange. But wherever two or three Bengalis meet there is a Bengali club. The quality is marked in Bengal by a tendency to do everything in groups, and outside by a tendency to keep apart from the rest of society. This makes for the preservation of the distinctive Bengali culture, which is a most marked feature of Bengali colonies throughout India, but also lessens their popularity in their adopted homes. Because the Bengalis were the first to take up Western education in northern India they for a time enjoyed a virtual monopoly of professional posts; Mukarjis, Chatterjis, and Sens were to be found in all the northern cities as far as Peshawar before the Partition. Outside Pakistan these colonies, often in their third and fourth generations, continue and are slowly becoming assimilated to their provincial neighbours.

We may pass briefly by the Assamese, whose differing race is almost submerged by the cultural influence of Bengal, and the gentle Oriyas of Orissa, where Bengali cultural influence is also strong. Crossing India to the west we come to the hardy Marathas of the western hills. A small but wiry race, they sprang to fame with their resistance to the Moghul armies in the seventeenth century, and then for a time disputed the dominion of India with the British. They are a near-imperial race in character as well as achievement, for they have all the gifts of empire building except imagination and the ability to handle others. Their scattered dynasties mark the traces of their empire and today they play an important but not dominant part in the life of western India. Their spiritual home is Poona, four hours' electric rail journey from Bombay, where the subtle intellect of the Maratha Brahmin expands in numerous colleges, and exercises itself in innumerable impromptu clubs under the stars. It was no accident that at one time the rival leaders of the moderate and extreme sections of Indian nationalism were both Maratha Brahmins, both living in Poona and belonging to the same section of the same caste. The Maratha is tough in the American sense, physically and morally. He is a long-headed man; a man who will make bricks without straw if he thinks them worth making and not cry out for a load of straw in order to make one brick. He is sometimes crude and lacking in taste and not very sensitive to art. But he is a man for all that, a man who, if he cannot construct an enduring empire for himself, can effectively pull down those which others have made.

We now come to the Dravidian lands of the Tamilian, Andhra, Kannadiga, and Malayali. All these races, except for the Brahmin section, are of a darker hue than their northern brethren. The Tamilian is the characteristic inhabitant of Madras. The Tamil Brahmins are noted for their intellect, and have produced mathematicians of world reputation. To feats of pure reason they unite prodigies of memory so that it is not uncommon to find, in the lower reaches of the intellectuals, both the man who can argue about anything and the man who thinks he knows everything. The Tamilian unites a high degree of Western education and a fondness for the English language which extends to taxi-drivers and domestic servants with an orthodox conservatism which has made him the least permeable of all the Indian races to Western social influences. The Tamil gentleman with his saffron caste-marks and ceremonial turban, his silver-topped stick and his European clothes, is a dignified landmark in southern India. None surpasses him in dignity, intelligence, and courtesy, and few equal him in social conservatism and love of the old ways. The great temples of the south are mainly his work. The merchants of Madras are famous for their enterprise, and it is from these coasts that cultural influence has penetrated to the Far East in the past, and waves of industrial emigration in the last century have travelled to Burma and Africa. The Indian overseas problem is mainly a Tamil problem.

The Andhras stretch to the north and are now coming into prominence with the development of the new port of Vizagapatam. A gentler people than the Tamilians, they possess a poorer soil and have played a smaller part in history. Apt to be jealous of Tamil predominance, they too are an intelligent and cultured people who have played their part in Indian overseas enterprise. The Kannadigas of the Mysore plateau have shown their worth in the great development of modern Mysore, but in general they do not differ greatly from the two former peoples. The Malayalis on the west coast are distinguished by a special quality of enterprise and push. For centuries they have acted as middlemen between East and West in the spice trade, and today they are to be found all over India and wherever Indian trade is carried on. Notable among them are the Muslim Moplahs, descendants of Arab traders who have trafficked in Malabar since Roman times, and the Syrian Christians, whose origin dates back to the same period. Malabar is famous for its social customs, such as the rule of inheritance through sisters, which produces unexpected complications. Women have perhaps greater freedom than in any other part of India, and there is nowhere else where by placing a pot outside her door a wife can indicate to her husband that he is not wanted.

We have now touched on all the principal races except the dwellers in the mountains of the north. But these, for all their charm and interest, are not likely to play any large part in the life of the country. Taking them as a whole they are perhaps the most secluded people upon earth. They enjoy the happiness of having no history, for their real history is the interminable and inexorable struggle against overshadowing natural forces. They have seen successive invasions desolate the plains and pass them by, they have seen even the inquisitive and intruding European confined, except for occasional shooting parties, to a few main paths and hill stations. They may yet survive the destruction of world civilization in an atomic war to find themselves, to their surprise and bewilderment, the heirs of all the ages.

4
Hinduism

HINDUISM HAS BEEN LIKENED to a vast sponge, which absorbs all that enters it without ceasing to be itself. The simile is not quite exact, because Hinduism has shown a remarkable power of assimilating as well as absorbing; the water becomes part of the sponge. Like a sponge it has no very clear outline on its borders and no apparent core at its centre. An approach to Hinduism provides a first lesson in the 'otherness' of Hindu ideas from those of Europe. The Western love of definition and neat pigeon-holing receives its first shock, and also its first experience of definition by means of negatives. For while it is not at all clear what Hinduism is, it is clear that it is not many things with which it may be superficially compared. It is not, for example, a sect or a church in any Western sense. There is no general council which lays down doctrine, no episcopal bench or convocation or assembly which determines policy, no list of incumbents available in reference books, no set of rules to be found in manuals. Yet it is certainly a religion for all that. But it is not a religion in the usual Western sense. There are no dogmas to be accepted by all, no doctrines of universal application, there is no *quod semper, quod ubique, quod ab omnibus*. I may believe in God or I may not, I may believe in a way of salvation or not, I may have certain moral beliefs or not, I may have opinions about the nature of the universe or not, and still be a Hindu. Opinion then is not the criterion of Hinduism. Is it to be found in ceremonial? A man may perform ceremonies without number and recite texts without limit, but if he fails to observe certain rules of life they will be of no avail for he will not be considered a Hindu. Is it then a matter of duties and observance of rules only?

Here again there is no one thing necessary to salvation. Observance of rules without ceremonies will not do any more in the long run than ceremonies without rules. A man may show great laxity in his ceremonies provided he performs certain basic duties; he may be lax in his duties provided he is punctilious in ceremonies; he may show a certain slackness in both provided he neglects neither entirely. But if he does so he will fall out of the sponge so to speak and be no longer reckoned a Hindu. And what will happen to him then? The answer is—nothing overt, nothing violent, nothing immediate. Is there then no tribunal before which he can be brought, no Inquisition to judge him, no Court of Discipline to punish him, no penitents' bench on which to place him? The answer is again in the negative. The only authorities to judge him are his own caste fellows, the only judgement they can give is what they consider is 'done' in their group, and the only sanction they have is the opinion of their fellow-members. There is, in fact, no external sanction for Hindu practice, no Pope or Emperor, no ecclesiastical thunders or legal terrors. Hinduism rests essentially on public opinion. Not to be a Hindu means simply not being thought to be a Hindu, and this entails in the long run a series of other negatives which make life intolerable. The system works much as excommunication or an interdict did in the Middle Ages. Once these sentences were pronounced, their enforcement depended upon public opinion and their effectiveness declined as soon as belief in their efficacy waned. But it would be misleading to suppose that a man would be outcasted in India for the same cause that he would be excommunicated in Europe. The cause of the latter was usually doctrinal and sometimes moral: the cause of the former is not likely to be either unless one regards morals as synonymous with custom. For it is a breach of custom more than anything else which moves the Hindu leviathan.

Is Hinduism, then, simply a matter of custom—peculiar and complicated, but still custom? The answer again is in the negative. The customs would not hold together if they were merely customs, and represented no values, and the existence of values implies to formulate them. Does Hinduism, then, have a creed or a doctrine or a decalogue after all? The answer here is no longer purely negative. Hinduism contains values, but no one set of values; it possesses doctrines and ideas, but not one doctrine once for all delivered to the saints; it has not one decalogue, but many for its numerous sections. These are the things which give strength to the pure automatism of custom, these are the things for which a Hindu will die, as the customs are things for which he lives. Even customs are so closely identified with the ideas which they express as to enter the 'dying' class, as for example the practice of cow veneration and the refusal to eat beef, with the idea of the sacredness of life. But the distinction is there and can be made in theory if not always in practice. We have, then, a body of ideas, beliefs, and values, which together make up the mysterious amorphous entity which is called Hinduism. Each is present in some one part of Hinduism and few in every part. Any one can be dispensed with in any one section without forfeiting the title of Hinduism, and no item is absolutely essential. But some of each class must always be there. You can have all of the items in some of the parts or some of the items in all of the parts, but not none of the items in any of the parts. If one likens Hinduism to a ship, one can compare the castes with its water-tight compartments, the essential ideas with the steel framework, and special fixtures such as the engines, the bridge, the steering gear with those things which are present in some, but not all sections of Hinduism. It is an intimate mixture of all the component parts whose loss would involve the sinking of the ship, and so it is with Hinduism. Some modern ships are so finely constructed and carefully subdivided as to be deemed unsinkable, and the same claim is often made for Hinduism. Seamen know that such claims are only based on a calculation of known dangers and the known qualities of the vessel, and sociologists would do well to be equally cautious in the case of Hinduism.

We may regard Hinduism as a body of customs and a body of ideas, the two together having such pervasive power and defensive force as to absorb or to resist passively for centuries any system which comes in contact with it. It will be convenient to consider some basic customs and then some of the fundamental ideas.

The basic Hindu institution is caste. Space forbids a detailed considera-tion of the origin of caste, which is still a matter of controversy among Indologists and sociologists. Certain factors in its formation can be mentioned and this must suffice for our purpose. There is first the occupational factor. The four main divisions apparently existed among the early Aryan-speaking tribes, though they were not necessarily in their present order of estimation or completely hereditary and certainly not immutably fixed or rigidly exclusive. There is then the racial factor. The origin of the outcaste conception can clearly be traced in the distaste of the early Aryan for the habits and customs of the aboriginal inhabitants. Aryan opinions of the indigenous peoples were not flattering and found forcible expression. Linked with race is the colour factor. The early Aryans were ruddy-faced and fair-skinned, the people of the land were dark or very dark. The Sanskrit word for caste is *varna*[1] or colour. Even today fairness is much prized in Hindu society; there is rejoicing when a

[1] The word 'caste' derives from the Portuguese 'casta'—race or tribe.

fair-skinned baby appears in a dark-complexioned Hindu family, and corresponding disappointment when the reverse occurs. Recent scholars have emphasized the primitive factor of taboo; just as the Aryan would not touch the primitive tribesman, so the tribesman would not touch the Aryan. The idea of the pollution of touch was mutual and segregation an agreed policy. Then there was the factor of conquest, conquered communities often being allowed to exist as a lower caste instead of being exterminated, or a conquering barbarian race being admitted to a place of higher degree as the price of absorption into the Hindu system. The Chinese educated their conquerors by making them mandarins; the Indians embalmed theirs by making them separate castes. Finally, there was the factor of heredity, the tendency of a community scattered over vast spaces and in contact with strange peoples to preserve their culture by handing it down from father to son and making everything hereditary.

The four main divisions of Hinduism are the Brahmin or priest, the Kshatriya or warrior, the Vaisya or merchant, and the Sudra or labourer. The outcastes or exterior castes, those originally outside the main Hindu system, are now really a fifth division, the Hindu class of the 'underprivileged'. They have been the fifth wheel of the Hindu coach, avowedly unwanted but nevertheless taking a share of the weight. It may turn out to be the main work of Mahatma Gandhi to have achieved their general recognition as an integral part of the whole Hindu community by the device of calling them Harijans or People of God.

Each main caste was originally an occupational division, and each in the course of time has undergone an almost infinite process of subdivision both occupation-wise and province-wise. It is in this social development that real continuity in India is to be found. In Europe, national divisions and political organizations tend to persist while social organisms dissolve and change; in India, states are transitory and societies persist. There was an English state in 1066, but one would hardly be at home in Norman society; a modern Hindu would be quite at sea in eleventh-century Indian politics, but Hindu society would be recognizable and not altogether uncongenial. Today members of many castes can choose a wide range of occupation, and the public services in particular are open to all, but it would still be true to say that in the whole Hindu society caste is an indication of occupation. Not all Brahmins are priests, but all priests are Brahmins; a cultivator is not likely to be a successful shopkeeper, or a moneylender a practising farmer. The cutting across of traditional occupations is most obvious in the towns and amongst all those who have been in some degree westernized, but even there a bias is visible towards the modern version of the hereditary occupation. The Brahmin gravitates to all intellectual pursuits, the Kayasth (or writer) to government service, the Sens (hereditary doctors) to Western medicine, and the merchant castes to commerce and industry.

The next feature of caste is heredity. The social regulator of heredity is marriage, and it is therefore no surprise to find Hindu society bristling with marriage regulations. Every caste has its own rules, but in general it may be said that marriage is compulsory not only within the main group, but also within certain sub-groups. Within those groups again there are groups into which you must marry and groups into which you cannot marry. Thus, life is often very complicated for the young Hindu, and what the heart longs for is by no means always what the soul receives. The difficulty of satisfying a set of conditions, like turning the lock of a complicated safe, gives a clue to the custom of arranging marriages and arranging them early. The system could not last a generation without it. Modern relaxation takes the form of jumping some of the lesser barriers and of raising the age of marriage to the point when the parties can have a voice in their own disposal. Among the educated classes it can now be said that there is generally consultation, but by no means always consent by the parties concerned. Among the rest of the people traditional conditions substantially prevail.

Caste both commands and forbids what a Hindu shall do, and the former, though often less spectacular than the latter, is just as important in social life. The essential positive Hindu duties are to preserve the family unit and its caste customs, to perform the ceremonies necessary thereto, and to pass on the torch to the next generation. Hinduism is essentially a domestic culture and this is one reason why the citadel of orthodoxy is to be found among the women of all castes. The proper performance of ritual and the maintenance of custom is bound up with family status and self-respect. The restrictive side of caste custom has been the stock-in-trade of travellers, publicists, and missionaries for generations. It is important to remember that these restrictions are merely the reverse of the positive Hindu duties, for unless one does so they appear meaningless and merely absurd. If it is once realized that certain positive customs and habits, handed down for generations, convey the feeling of rightness and propriety to Hindus just as certain customs, like the rules of cricket or baseball, convey the same feeling to Englishmen or Americans, a great barrier to the understanding of the Hindu mind is removed. If an Englishman objects to shooting foxes because it is 'unsporting', why should not a Hindu object to killing them at all because it conflicts with the principle of the sacredness of life? In both cases the objection rests on the same basis—the act proposed offends the subject's sense of rightness or propriety.

From this point of view the inhibitions or 'prejudices' of Hindus can be more objectively considered. Apart from marriage they chiefly affect touch, food, and the taking of life. Restrictions of touch arise from the principle of ceremonial purity and specially concern the relations of the upper castes with 'untouchables'. They also concern the receiving of food by one community from another. They have produced the curious anomaly of a demand for Brahmin cooks, since Brahmins are the only community whose touch cannot defile anyone else. These restrictions tend to be blunted by modern conditions, specially by that great leveller the railway, but in broad outline they remain. On every railway station and in every institution Hindu and Muslim water-pots were a familiar feature, each dispensed by its own attendant. Food restrictions are bound up with Hindu ideas of the sacredness of life in general and of the cow, a kind of specialized symbol of all fruitfulness, in particular. Thus, no Hindu will eat beef, even those who become Christians often retaining an instinctive aversion to it, and only some will eat any other kind of meat. Emancipated Hindus who face mutton without blenching will stop short at beef. Fish in general comes under the ban, though in Bengal it is conveniently regarded as a marine vegetable. Once fairly launched on vegetarianism a fresh vista of distinction becomes possible. There are the egg-eaters and the abstainers—is not a fertile egg a form of life?—the pro- and anti-onion parties, and those who consider beetroot too suggestive in colour for respecters of life to approve. Finally, the life-principle finds expression not only in a general disinclination to take life even of aged and diseased animals and a tendency to leave nature alone, but in a particular veneration for such unprofitable creatures as monkeys and peacocks and ants.

There remain certain other features of Hindu society without which even this cursory survey would be incomplete. The first is the Hindu joint family, an institution known to the Muslims also. The single and separate families of Western society are repugnant to traditional Hindu feelings; they seem lonely and selfish and forlorn. The typical Hindu family is a group of families living together, recognizing the patriarchal authority of the eldest member, having a common purse and a highly developed family feeling. The sons bring their wives back to the family fold, where they are subject to the family matriarch and the children mix together in a crowd. The son's earnings commonly go into the family coffers from which he receives an allowance, and he is *per contra* supported should he be unemployed. The whole tendency is towards dependence on the family manager, while of privacy there is little or none. The institution has very important social consequences whose understanding is essential for a grasp of Hindu society. The first is the emergence of a limited number of outstanding personalities, exercising despotic sway with more or less kindliness, and accustomed to dispose of the lives of dependants without any great regard for their wishes or susceptibilities. 'What's for their good, not what pleases them' is the rule of the typical Hindu joint family. No note of democracy here, as the Hindu college youth often finds to his cost and ruefully admits in private. The system produces women equally outstanding, benevolent or perverse, according to inclination.

Apart from the patriarchs and matriarchs the system promotes a spirit of dependence, and retards initiative and enterprise. Reverence for parental and family authority weighs heavily on the young man anxious to strike out a new line and tends to arrest character development in its most susceptible and formative years. Reliance on family support saps the sense of responsibility and turns many a potential steady worker into a drifter. Every educationist knows how many promising careers are nipped in the bud and budding characters blighted by family pressure far stronger than anything known in the West, and too strong not only for weak, but often also for average and sensitive natures. The fruits of the system are seen in a docility and lack of enterprise which are a standing puzzle to the foreign observer. Another feature is a family patriotism which places the welfare of the family member before that of the public. This persists even where families have formally broken up under the stress of modern life, and is the root cause of the nepotism noticeable in public life. In Hinduism nothing matters really, so long as the family flourishes. But the joint family has also its advantages. If there is no privacy, there is a wonderful capacity for living together without friction, for making the best of things. There is great devotion among the family members, and often a willingness to sacrifice for the general good which would make a Westerner blush. If there is sometimes narrowness and tyranny, there is often a tranquil and affectionate community life which might well be the envy of the more fevered dwellers in more temperate climes.

The family brings us to the Hindu woman, whose graceful and flowing colourful dress charms every Westerner in India and assures her of a welcome in the West. The Hindu woman has a distinct place in Hindu

society, but it is a distinctly subordinate place. She is worshipped as a
mother, venerated as a wife, loved as a sister, but not much regarded as a
woman. Woman as woman is the handmaid of man; her duty is to worship
her husband, to bear and rear his children. Her position as woman is
shown by what happens to her when her husband is dead. As a woman
she has significance only in relation to man. For this reason every woman
is married at an early age and though the general rule of monogamy
prevails (except for rajahs) a man could take a second wife if the first had
no children. Her property rights were vested in her husband, and she had
very limited rights of inheritance. Marriage was sacramental and indis-
soluble, so that on the husband's death there was nothing left for the
widow but to await reunion with her husband. This is the basis of the
Hindu custom of widowhood, and of *sati* the practice of immolation on
the funeral pyre of the husband. The ideal woman is Sita, who followed
her husband into exile, remained faithful when kidnapped, was rescued,
and then voluntarily left him at the first breath of scandal, in order to
protect his reputation. Such sacrifice is admirable in Hindu eyes and no
one has ever criticized Rama for letting her go. But if a woman is significant only in relation to man, since she is related to him a great deal, she
has a very considerable significance. One must beware of assuming that
subordinate significance means no significance at all, for this would be a
travesty of the truth. A woman's position really depends upon her family
status; her importance waxes and wanes with the fluctuations of the
family fortunes, not in terms of money, but of children, daughters-in-law,
and so on. But within that unit her influence is very great and often
salutary. In the past there was no escape for the Hindu woman from the
family circle, except by becoming a courtesan or a *sanyasin* or ascetic.
Today the professions are open to those who will enter them, and a
rapidly increasing number are seeking both Western education and the
independence for which it gives a taste. Like their brothers, Hindu
college-bred girls often find the conflict acute between Western ideas of
personality and liberty and traditional notions of dependence and sub-
ordination. The Hindu widow is one of the social problems of India.
There is nothing left for her but to think of her husband, and to become
the family drudge; she is banished from even Hindu society. Well-to-do
families keep their widows out of sight, but even here there are many
suicides and runaways. The poor are practically slaves unless they become
devotees at a shrine (as thousands do) or seek more gaudy relief. Widow
schools and remarriage societies have so far only touched the fringe of
the problem.

There remains the great class of 50 millions outside the Hindu fold known socially as outcastes, ceremonially as untouchables, bureaucratically as depressed classes or scheduled castes, scientifically as the exterior castes, and by Mr. Gandhi as Harijans or People of God. Spread all over India it may be said that in general they perform all the menial work of the Hindu community, from scavenging to certain kinds of craftsmanship. In general they are the descendants of conquered aboriginals whom the Hindus preferred to enslave rather than to kill. The slavery is of the mind, the conviction that they are morally and spiritually inferior and that their only hope of improvement in another life consists in the patient performance of menial duties in this. These people commonly live segregated, in both town and country, but their conditions vary greatly, from the comparative freedom and physical vigour of the Punjab to the extreme squalor of the south where a Polyar could not approach within ninety-six paces of a Nambudri Brahmin and had to make dismal noises to give warning of his polluting approach. A group of 'unseeables' was still recorded in the 1931 census. In western India the sturdy Mahars formed valuable units of the Indian army until orthodox Maratha prejudice led to their disbandment. More than Mr. Gandhi's sermons the social hurly-burly of modern industrial cities is doing something to break up the system, both by opening new avenues of employment, including technical ones, and by making the observance of untouchability more and more difficult for the castes. There is no untouchability in an Indian third-class railway carriage.

The ideas which underlie the Hindu social system are even more important than the system itself, for the system is largely their social expression and on their continued acceptance depends the durability of Hinduism in the modern world. If we wish to judge of the adaptability of Hinduism, or of its suitability for the conditions of a modern industrialized society, we must consider the validity of Hindu ideas in the light of modern thought. There are four Hindu conceptions which may be briefly considered. They are *dharma*, *varna*, *maya*, and *karma*.

Dharma may be roughly equated with duty, *varna* means colour and so caste, *maya* signifies illusion, and *karma*, the doctrine of consequences. Each may be considered in turn, beginning with the last.

Karma is the logical doctrine of moral consequences. Every action good or bad has its consequences and each consequence must be fully worked out. There are no short-cuts away from the consequences of evil; repentance may bring forgiveness in the sense of excusing the guilt, but will not avert the consequences. It is these consequences which are the atonement for the act. Similarly, a man cannot achieve merit without incurring thereby the inevitable consequences. So logical and rigorous a doctrine demands a wider stage than the span of a single life, and this is provided by the doctrine of transmigration of souls, which is essential to the working of *karma*. We are not isolated individuals, creatures of a moment, flying in and out of the hall of life like King Ethelbert's sparrow, but a link in a potentially endless chain of lives. Whether that chain is a conveyor-belt which endlessly repeats a certain cycle, as Plato thought, is not relevant; the essential point is that each life is only one of a series, with a before and after. The fact of life remains, the content of life depends upon the will and behaviour of the individual. By resolute endeavour and suitable exercises a man may ultimately escape from the chain into direct union with the One, but this is a long and laborious process, the goal so far of the favoured few. Apart from this our position in this life is determined by the past, and our position in the next partly by the past and partly by one's own efforts. This conception gives a curiously timeless quality to the Hindu's mind. For him life is an endless process of which he is now enjoying one fleeting glimpse of many, not, as for both ancient and modern European agnostics, a window of eternity out of which one can look for a time, and be gone. Nothing is irretrievably lost and nothing on the moral plane is certainly gained; it is all a nicely calculated less or more. On the other hand, it makes for pessimism and despair in personal relations, for reincarnation, while making continuance certain, renders the meeting of loved ones and their recognition matters of popular doubt. *Karma* makes for ultimate certainty, but reduces incentive to immediate effort; it guarantees continuity, but reduces the sense of urgency and blunts the spur to action; above all it gives the Hindu a different attitude to time from our own, an attitude which colours all his thoughts and influences all his actions. A Hindu does not see time passing him by, he flows with it, like a boat on a river. Periodically he changes boats, but the voyage continues.

The next idea is of *dharma*, or duty, which is intimately bound up with that of caste. If *karma* explains a man's position in the caste network, *dharma* tells him what to do in that position. *Dharma* does not coincide with the Western idea of duty, since it is not related to any fixed principle, but it resembles the Western code in that it carries with it a sense of moral obligation, so that failure is a moral fault. The duty of a caste may be immoral from the Western point of view, and also from that of another caste, but it would nevertheless be immoral for a member of that caste to neglect it. The so-called criminal tribes come under that category, for cattle-lifting and the like are to them a duty. In the same way the Thugs, as devotees of the goddess Kali, thought it their duty to strangle w..yfarers as an offering to the goddess. These may be called perversions, but to use this word would be to misunderstand the whole nature of *dharma*. My *dharma* is the occupation and behaviour fitting to my caste and it is my moral duty to follow the rules of that caste and no others through life. So the moneylender is expected to be a keen businessman and the warrior a brave soldier. The moneylender has no call to be brave or the warrior to be keen-witted; if he is so, it is a credit item in his spiritual account, a work of supererogation, but no blame attaches to the absence of virtues outside the prescribed list. The idea of *dharma* is not of course rigidly applied, and it would be easy to find exceptions. But it runs through the whole of Hindu thought and practice, and is an essential part of Hindu mental processes. Thus, every occupation, including government service and the professions, has its own duties and obligations which a man cannot ignore without loss of esteem. The idea of duty has been cut up into packets and distributed among the groups and professions, and in the process its connexion with moral principles has been blurred and sometimes lost altogether.

Finally, there comes *maya*, or illusion. In the background of the endless round of death and rebirth, the inexorable working out of consequences and its corollary the caste system, and the infinite variations upon the themes 'My station and its duties' which are called *dharma*, lies the fundamental question—*To what end?* Hindu thought is saturated with theism. Sceptical theories certainly exist, but on any large scale they just cannot breathe in the Indian air. But Hinduism is not only theistic; it is also pantheistic. There is an ever-present tendency to identify God with Nature, the One with the Universe. The West is apt to think the world more real than God, so that Voltaire could say that if God did not exist it would be necessary to invent him—in order to make the world; so that Hegel thought of God, along with the Universe, as in the process of becoming, while Renan could be described as thinking that God would like to exist if he could; India thinks of God as more real than the world. There is no ultimate purpose in life but eventual reunion with the One, and all doctrines, disciplines, devotions, and ecstasies are but means to that end. The world is part of God, but not the whole of him; it is his thought or dream, 'the baseless fabric of his vision', and ultimately has no substance at all. Man, to obtain Union, must escape from the round of births and deaths, from the chains of passion and desire. He escapes by realizing that actuality is illusion, by purging the passions because they lead to action and so create the strong delusion from which he wishes to be free. 'Decay is inherent in all compounded things.'[1] The fever called living is to the Hindu really a fever and not a more or less pleasant unique reality. *Moksha*, or freedom, to the Hindu is freedom from action, from desire, and from the material world. These ideas, it should be emphasized, are not merely philosophic theories fit only for the lecture-room or the hermit's cave. They are of the texture of the Hindu mind, something with which the Hindu lives, something which is part of him. The consequence is that Hinduism is a world-renouncing system rather than, like Christianity, a world-accepting one. The world is for ever too much with the Hindu. He lacks much incentive to change it now, because he always looks forward to another change in the future. *Moral* behaviour in this life will bring material as well as moral improvement in the next. But why bother so much about improving the world if your real object is to get away from it all by realizing that it is only a dream? The background conviction that the material world is an illusion tends to produce a static state of mind indifferent to material progress. It creates that shrinking from the material as something evil which is the so-called spirituality of India; it is responsible for the Hindu knack of argument by negation and action by non-co-operation which puzzles and irritates those nurtured in the activist Greek tradition of the West. The Hindu respects the rajah, but venerates the ascetic, because the ascetic personifies renunciation and is following what every Hindu in his heart believes to be the only true way of life. There may seem to be little spirituality about some types of merchants in India, but for all their love of money they accept the idea of renunciation as the greatest good; that is why the Hindu either tends to despise the material altogether, or to collect his goods without taste or reason. If he looks on them at all he regards them quantitatively not qualitatively, for the simple reason that he does not associate the idea of value with material goods. So art and beauty are left to the connoisseur and the hereditary craftsman for whom it is a *dharma*, or moral duty, to be practised, not for the sake of cultivating beauty, but because it is the duty assigned by Providence to his station in life.

In sum we may say that these ideas equip the Hindu with a set of values quite distinct from those of the West, and it is these values which form the core of his socio-religious system. Many details, no doubt, have grown up by the mere accretion of custom, and these may be modified by the adoption of new customs like the modern fashion of looking to the West. But the main structure will not change until the ideas themselves

[1] *Dhammapada, or Way of Virtue*, p. 71.

are transmuted. A fungus here or a parasite there may be removed, a dead branch or broken twig may be lopped off, but the Hindu tree of life will stand so long as the sap of Hindu ideology continues to rise. This is the great question before Hinduism today—to prune and cut, or to replant altogether, to change or not to change? Can Western ideas be grafted on to the parent Hindu stem, or must there be a fresh planting altogether?

5
Islam

GIBBON DEFINED THE MUSLIM CREED as a great truth and a necessary falsehood. The student of politics in India might call it a great fact and a necessary division. It is necessary first to realize that the Muslim community exists and has an independent existence, and then that it is essentially different in texture and outlook from the Hindu community. Muslims are not mere exceptions here and there to the general rule of Hinduism; they are a large and compact body of people who exist in their own right and have to be considered independently of the Hindus. They are not simply people of a different religious denomination, as Methodists might differ from Roman Catholics; they are not people who go to different churches yet have a common culture and the same national outlook. They are sufficiently different to consider themselves a separate nation; they differ from the Hindus not only in belief, but also in culture, traditions, and, above all, in their sense of values. A Methodist may feel at home with a Roman Catholic on almost everything except theology and worship, but a Muslim must make an effort to feel at home with a Hindu on anything outside business. Dress, customs, food, codes of conduct, and ideals are all different, and it is only when these have been successfully relegated to the background that the average Muslim can be at ease with the average Hindu.

Having said so much, we must beware of going too far. Muslims should not be denied the name of Indian. For there is one thing, in spite of all their differences, which they share—the Indian temperament and love of the soil. The Muslim Bengali has much the same temperament as his Hindu neighbour, though their ideas and customs differ radically. Similarly, Punjabi Hindus share with Muslims the Punjabi temperament, as is shown by such common tastes as love of sport and love of a fight.

A European parallel may be suggested in the northern and southern Irishman, and perhaps still more in the southern Catholic and southern Protestant, where there is emphatic conscious difference in almost every respect, but an equally emphatic affinity of temperament. Another parallel is that of French and British Canadians. Here temperament as well as tastes and opinions differ, but there is an underlying consciousness of belonging to the new world, and a common pride in being Canadian. The point to be grasped is that while the Muslim is a different species of Indian from the Hindu, he is an Indian for all that. He may look outside for help, but he has no longing to go outside to live; he may look to Arabia for inspiration, but he prefers Hindustan for its expression. Geographical India is his home, India the scene of his hopes and fears.

The initial contrast with Hinduism which strikes the observer is one of definiteness. If Hinduism may be compared to a cloud with its vague outlines and uncertain amorphous composition, Islam may be likened to a water-tower with its sharply defined shape and its very definite contents. You become aware of Hinduism by its atmosphere; you can tell Islam by its definite attributes. You become damp in a cloud; you record the shape of the water-tower and measure the water which flows from it. You feel Hinduism; you catalogue Islam. Thus, one says of Hinduism that certain things are to be found within it, but none of these things in themselves can be called Hinduism *per se*; with Islam one can take certain characteristics and say without hesitation, 'This is Islam.' These characteristics are, briefly, a Creed, a Book, and a Brotherhood. The creed is that of the Prophet—'There is no god but God and Mohammad is his prophet'; the book is the Koran, which contains both dogma and rule of life; and the Brotherhood is the equality of all Muslims before God and to each other. This first distinction shows at once why Islam and Muslims are commonly more easily understood by Westerners than are Hindus and Hinduism. Christianity also has a Creed, a Book, and a Brotherhood, and though the characteristics of each differ widely from those of Islam there is a common approach to life, a common way of looking at things, which makes the Westerner and the Muslim feel more akin. Muslims and Christians both accept the world and seek to make the best of it; they have a creed about it and rules for living in it. Hindus do not accept the world, but seek to escape from it; they have a creed which denies its existence and rules to get out of it. For Muslims and Christians life is a probation for the next world and therefore supremely important; for the Hindu it is 'doing time' in illusion and therefore without ultimate significance.

The Muslims in India numbered 96 millions out of a total population of 388 millions, according to the census of 1941. There may be some reason for doubting the accuracy of the 1941 figures since the relation of numbers to Assembly seats caused great efforts to inflate totals, but as both sides were equally energetic, the proportion of Muslims to the whole is probably accurate enough. The strength of the Muslim community was not, however, in exact proportion to their numbers. Dispersion sapped their strength and was indeed one of the fundamental causes of the communal problem. If the Muslims had been a compact body in a particular area, like Ulstermen in Northern Ireland, some sort of division would have been comparatively easy, as it was in Ireland. But in fact, apart from certain areas of strength, Muslims were scattered all over the sub-continent, generally as a small minority. Even in the majority areas the majorities were not always overwhelming.

There are two main bodies of Muslims and a number of smaller groups. The first compact body is in the north-west, which forms what may be called the main Pakistan country. This region covers the tribal area of Baluchistan, the province of Sind, the North-West Frontier, the Punjab as far as the Sutlej, and the State of Bahawalpur. Adjacent to it lies the disputed territory of Kashmir. Here dwell what may be called the fighting Muslims, people with martial traditions, physical vigour, and sometimes of foreign descent. The second area of concentration is Eastern Pakistan, comprising eastern Bengal and the plains of Assam, with its spiritual centre in Dacca. The people here differ racially in no way from their Hindu neighbours. Apart from these two areas, which now constitute Pakistan, there are a number of Muslim *enclaves* among the Hindu population. Thus in the north the great cities like Delhi, Agra, and Lucknow have substantial Muslim elements, and there are patches of Muslim settlement like the Rohillas (Afghans by descent) in Oudh and the Syeds of Barha. In the south there are substantial groups in Andhra State, and down the west coast from Gujarat to Travancore, including Bombay. For the rest there is a sprinkling of Muslims everywhere, more marked in the country than in the towns.

It is usually assumed that the majority of Muslims represent the 'conquerors of India' in past ages. In fact, this is not the case, and it is well to be clear at the outset that the great majority of Muslims in India are Indians of Indian descent. Nevertheless their origins are diverse, and some understanding of them helps in estimating the complexity both of their composition and of their relations with the Hindus. The first group comes, of course, from the invading armies from the north-west.

The word armies is used advisedly, for the Muslim invasions were distinguished from some of the earlier ones by the fact that they were not folk migrations, like the Teutonic and later the Slav movements in Europe. They were the forays of raiding parties or the invasions of regular armies, and, as such, except perhaps in the north-west, they did not make large-scale settlements on the land. From the beginning these men formed a military and political governing caste, and though their numbers were big enough to form communities, they were professional and, so, scattered groups rather than agricultural and compact bodies. These men and their descendants formed first a military aristocracy, then a ruling class, and finally a social élite.[1] Their traces can be seen today in the best Muslim families. It is a distinction, for example, to be a Qureishi, or a member of the Arab tribe of the prophet Mohammad, a Syed or direct descendant of the Prophet, a Moghul or descendant of the northern adventurers of the sixteenth century, a Chagatai Turk, or an Afghan. The name Bokhari is an honoured surname, because it implies descent from the Turks of Bokhara in central Asia. This point is emphasized by the eagerness of aspiring families to annex an ancient patronymic. But when we have got so far, we have only accounted for a proportion of the ninety-six millions. In fact, the majority are of Hindu descent. Some of these are no doubt the result of forcible conversions. Periods occurred when this was done on a considerable scale, but in general it was a sporadic process resorted to in times of excitement such as the capture of a city and the looting of towns in the first flush of victory. Taken as a whole, Indian history has been remarkable for the clemency extended to the vanquished in war and for the regard shown to women and children. Amongst the many exceptions which prove the general rule, Taimur's execution of 100,000 Hindu captives in a moment of panic before Delhi in 1398 may be matched by the record of raiding Marathas in the eighteenth century and of the brigand Pindaris in the early years of the nineteenth. Owing to the ceremonial peculiarities of Hinduism, forcible conversion was curiously easy. Bring a Brahmin into contact with beef, for example, and he felt himself to be for ever cut off from his kind; the profession of Islam was then the only, and by no means intolerable, alternative to joining the ranks of the outcastes.

In fact, however, the majority of conversions were of two kinds, individual among the upper-class Hindus, and mass among the lower. Many individuals among the upper classes have embraced Islam through the centuries, and some old-established Muslim families retain their

[1] See Chap. 6, on Muslim invasions.

Hindu names in pride of their Brahmin descent. Some changed their faith from conviction and others from policy; a list could be made of high Muslim ministers who were Hindu converts. Office was often worth a mosque, as Paris was once worth a mass. But the bulk supply, as it were, came from two main sources. All over India, but specially where the Muslims were firmly established in power or in considerable numbers this creed attracted the Hindu outcaste. Its promise of brotherhood, its simple and concrete demands, its comparatively few taboos, opened up a new world to any outcaste who could see beyond the mud walls of his village; and it is perhaps only the rural isolation of India as a whole, together with the absence of effective Muslim power in large areas, which has prevented the absorption by Islam of the whole outcaste community. In eastern India another factor was at work. Bengal was the last resort of a popular if decayed Buddhism. Not long before the Muslim conquest the Buddhist was replaced by a militant Hindu dynasty, the traditional opponents of Buddhism. Thus, conditions resembled those in the Middle East before the appearance of Mohammad, and the Buddhists were inclined to welcome the Muslims as deliverers, as heretical Christians welcomed the Arabs in the seventh century. Not force but a release from tension made a Muslim of the eastern Bengali. There is one more factor, that of peaceful penetration along the west coast of India. Arab traders had their settlements from the discovery of the working of the monsoons in the first century and in due course became Muslims. These settlements multiplied by intermarriage and became indigenous Muslim communities in a predominantly Hindu country.

The nature of Hinduism made it necessary to describe the customs first and to infer from them the underlying ideas; the nature of Islam makes it simpler to define ideas and beliefs first and consider the customs afterwards. What then must a man do to be a Muslim? He must first repeat the Muslim creed, 'There is no god but God and Mohammad is his prophet,' and he should submit to the rite of circumcision. These are the two hallmarks of Islam. Belief in Mohammad means acceptance of his mission and so of his teaching which is enshrined in the Koran, and this involves certain theological, moral, and personal consequences. These are to be found in the three great systems of Muslim doctrine, Muslim morality, and Muslim law.

The essence of Muslim doctrine is the unity and transcendence of God. The unity of God makes the Trinity highly suspect if not incomprehensible to the Muslim, and the multiple gods of the popular Hindu pantheon positively repulsive. Its obverse side is the passionate rejection of idolatry, and though this may have been originally a Semitic character-istic, it is now thoroughly acclimatized in India. A temple is an idol house, dedicated to devils. Along with this goes an equal objection to the fertility aspect of popular Hinduism as specially manifested in the Siva cult. The transcendence of God involves an almost equally emphatic denial of the idea of divine incarnation. What in Christianity is the great exception which proves the rule of human frailty is endemic in Hinduism, so here is another great matter of difference. God, as the theologians would say, is completely 'other' to the Muslim; he is high and lifted up, and who can attain unto him? The Hindu doctrine that God and the soul in man are identical is thus rank blasphemy to the Muslim.

From the creed we pass to the moral and ceremonial code. In many points the Muslim code resembles the Christian, for it has common origins. Mohammad borrowed heavily from the Jews, with whom he was in contact in Arabia. The Arabs in the great days of the Caliphate carried on the torch of Greek philosophy and imbibed the Aristotelian theory of justice. From these two systems many characteristics of Islamic law and practice derive and it is perhaps worth while to enumerate some of them briefly. The Jewish idea of fasting has found expression in the institution of the annual month of fasting called Ramzan, during which time no water or food may be taken from sunrise to sunset. As the Muslim calendar is lunar, this entails real hardship when the fast falls in the hot weather. The fast is still almost universally observed by Muslims in India. The Jewish Sabbath found its place in the Muslim observance of Friday as the day of congregational prayer. A visit to any large mosque on a Friday will demonstrate the abiding reality of this institution. From Judaism, also, comes the Muslim idea of clean and unclean meats, particularly the prohibition of pork. The Judaic law is also influential in the personal law of Islam enshrined in the Traditions of the Prophet and the *Shariat*. To the Greeks, as one would expect, the Muslims are more indebted for ideas than for rules. Their ideas of God, of justice, of science, are all influenced from this source. Muslim medicine is a direct carry-over from the Greek system, and to this day it is known as the Yunani (or Greek) system. Muslim mathematics continued where the Greeks left off.

But not everything Muslim is Greek or Jewish; Arabia has also its part in the Indian Muslim's heritage. The prohibition of spirits, genuine among the rank and file, but by no means universal among the upper classes, is of Arabian origin. So is the prohibition of music in worship, though it is popular enough in other respects. So also is the banishment of all representation of living forms from art, a decree which has proved effectual in sculpture and architecture if not altogether in painting. Islam has its sacred language of Arabic and its special ritual of prayer in the mosques. But the greatest of these Arab contributions has been in the matter of sexual morality. The Prophet himself allowed a limit of four wives, and perhaps because he himself overstepped the limit in later life, Islamic law recognizes the institution of concubinage or subordinate wives. In actual practice there is very little difference between Muslim and Hindu ruling princes and landed magnates in this respect, nor is there much in the lower and middle classes, for economic reasons. Plurality of wives is feasible only for the well-to-do who can afford their maintenance, and it can be said that among these the practice is declining because it is looked upon with increasing disfavour as being out of tune with the times. A second wife may be taken to remedy the lack of male heirs or under an infatuation when a man reaches 'the dangerous age'. But when all these 'set-offs' have been allowed, there remains no doubt that the institution tends to undermine the position of Muslim womanhood. In many respects the Muslim woman is, on paper, freer than her Hindu sister. Marriage being a contract, not a sacrament, divorce exists and a woman may divorce a man as well as a man a woman. The woman as well as the man can also remarry. She has property rights distinct from her husband and a specified share in inheritance. A Muslim woman can be a person of substance in her own right. There are not wanting those amongst the poorer classes who exploit this institution of divorce by making a regular trade of decoying husbands and then decamping with the dowry. To get free the man must divorce the woman, who can then repeat the process. But this freedom for Muslim women is in India mainly on paper only. There can be little doubt that the position of the Hindu married woman is on the whole preferable so long as her husband is alive. This is due partly to theological considerations and partly to the institution of *purdah* or seclusion. Though the Hindu woman is not respected as a woman, she is significant in respects in which nearly all women share —as a sister, wife, and mother. She must worship her husband as a god, but she should be worshipped by her children as a goddess. The Muslim doctrine of women is much more severe. Without arguing the question of the female soul, it is clear that the woman is regarded as subordinate to, and mainly as a convenience of, man; and she is so frail, or such a temptation, that she must be kept apart from male society. She has no touch of divinity as with the Hindus. She cannot enter even the public part of a mosque to pray. The result of this is seen in the traditional failure to educate Muslim women, which means in turn that they cannot enjoy their large legal rights under Muslim law, firstly because they hardly know of their existence, and secondly because they possess no independent means of livelihood.

The seclusion of women was not enjoined by Mohammad, nor is it practised in all Muslim countries. But it certainly exists in India and is too prominent a feature to be passed over. In the Punjab it is not practised in the villages except in the presence of total strangers, but it is an almost universal custom in the towns. The seclusion of women may be described as a social tunnel. The poorest classes have not the means, financial or material, to compass it; a step forward in the social march and it is a point of honour to enter the tunnel; at the furthest reach one emerges again into the light of general society. Seclusion and lack of education mean ill-health, ignorance, superstition, and apathy; education, on its side, is apt to mean revolt against seclusion. Tuberculosis is rampant among the secluded women of the towns, and affections of the eyes are caused by the curious cotton grille in the white shroud which Muslim women should wear when in public, and through which they have to peer.

In social life the Muslim has his own dress and modes of address; if you cannot tell a Muslim by his clothes you can always rely on his mode of salutation. To some extent Muslim court dress and court manners spread all over India, as the influence of Versailles radiated all over Europe, but modern Hindus tend to substitute European manners and ceremonial dress, so making the distinction easier. The Muslim loves sport of every kind, from big-game shooting to cock-fighting, pigeon-training, and kite-flying. He is a social being and lover of the good things of life. He delights in feasts and loves poetry, which he cultivates in poetical assemblies where rival poets declaim variations on set themes. Many men will quote the Persian poets or voice classical Urdu songs on the slightest provocation; it is as if London taxi-drivers drove the streets with Elizabethan lyrics on their lips. His religion is mainly a matter of outward observance, but in this he is punctilious. Often on weekdays, usually on Fridays, and always on great days, the serried ranks of white-robed worshippers may be seen prostrating themselves in unison. The creed and the ceremonial emphasize the brotherhood, the brotherhood and the customs both promote unity and mark off the Muslims from the rest of the world. The Muslim as a believer in the one God has a unity of spirit with his fellows unknown to the Hindu, and it is this above all which has prevented his absorption by the Hindu sponge.

With over seven centuries of contact and conflict it would seem inevitable that the two systems must influence each other. In fact, their wide differences have made their mutual influence much less than might have been expected; the principle of repulsion has been more obviously at work than that of attraction. The Muslim influence has been mainly theological and the Hindu mainly social, each being most effective where its expression is most vigorous. The unity and moral character of God has been the side of Islam which has impressed the Hindu, and it has stimulated a series of reform movements prompted by the idea of mutual comprehension. All these movements, of which Sikhism is the largest, emphasize the unity of God and his demands on man, and all their leaders—of whom perhaps Kabir, the Muslim weaver of Benares, was the most eloquent—enjoin worship and moral practice above ritual or social custom. Most of these movements (again including Sikhism) condemn idolatry. On the Muslim side, Hindu pantheistic philosophy with its neglect of forms and distrust of the material, its tendency to identify God and Nature, its disregard of moral distinctions, has largely influenced the Muslim mystics or Sufis. In the sphere of religious practice a notable borrowing has been the habit of reverencing saints and, indeed, the dead generally. Lights are burnt, flowers are offered, as if at a Hindu shrine, and this tends to happen not only to recognized 'saints', but to kings or anyone else whose tombs happen to come handy to the devotee. But perhaps the biggest loan from Hinduism is the practice of caste. It is true that Muslims in general would repudiate any such intention, and certainly the ideas behind caste are absent. But the idea of caste in its aspect of marriage restriction undoubtedly is to be found in the Muslim community. There are groups of Muslims who are almost as exclusive as separate castes, and in the lower classes are found many borrowings from Hindu customs which often are a mere continuation from Hindu times. But there is always the difference, perhaps vital, that such customs have social but not religious sanction, that their breach does not exclude from the Muslim brotherhood, and that all are united before God and in a crisis.

What are the things which keep Muslims and Hindus apart, which make them feel that they are different races and nations, which keep them permanently potentially on edge with each other? The first perhaps is the doctrinal issue of idolatry. The Muslim has borrowed from the Semitic races both his passionate rejection of polytheism and his passionate hatred of idolatry. A Muslim has not only an opinion about idolatry, but a deep-seated feeling, an instinct which affects his whole outlook on life. The worship of many gods, the portrayal of the divine in human form, is something to him which is less than human, the mark of the beast. It has, I think, no counterpart in the West; for it is far stronger than our ideas of good form or fair play or the behaviour of a gentleman. The nearest analogy in Western experience is, perhaps, that of obscenity. The ramifications of these emotions are widespread through the whole realm of Hindu-Muslim relations because of the ubiquitous working of the Hindu doctrine of incarnation. So much in Hinduism is divine. The Muslim does not mind a Hindu not eating beef, for example, but he does object to his worshipping the cow. In times of irritation there is consequently a strong urge to kill a cow out of sheer bravado.

On the side of social custom the chief irritant among Muslims is the caste system in general and the claims of the Brahmins in particular. These claims offend the strong Muslim sense of equality and repel by their exclusiveness. The Muslim taboo of pork is another sore point in social relations, for though it is not a food of caste Hindus any more than of Muslims, its defiling effect makes it an easy subject for provocation. So, too, does the Muslim prohibition of music in worship. Pork in the mosque or music outside are certain ways of provoking a Hindu-Muslim riot.

But the mental anguish of mutual relations is not all on the Muslim side. Hindus suffer acutely in the ceremonial sphere. Hindu feelings about the cow are as untranslatable into Western terms as are Muslim feelings about idolatry, and they are no less strong. A Hindu may literally turn sick at the sight or smell of beef. Muslim practice in the matter of food seems to the typical Hindu to be impure, dirty, and degraded, something beneath the level of man. He cannot understand, on the other hand, what he calls Muslim fanaticism on the subject of idolatry. Orthodox Hindu and Muslim individuals can be, and often are, very good friends, but they usually take good care that their intercourse avoids these danger areas. The mined waters of the Indian social ocean are numerous and intricate and by no means clearly buoyed, and it is no wonder that not only the oblivious European, but sometimes Indians themselves suffer sudden shipwreck thereon.

These are some of the abiding sources of Hindu-Muslim misunderstanding, which are inherent in the two systems. To these must be added two subsidiary factors which happened to be potent recently. The first was economic rivalry. The Hindu was a financier and businessman, the Muslim in general an agriculturist and soldier. So it happened that the Muslim was frequently in debt to the Hindu and had something of the feeling of the agricultural Arab towards the Zionist Jew in Palestine. The Hindu was the man who 'did' him. This issue was vital in the matter of industrialization, since most of the industrial resources and nearly all the capital and skill of united India were in the hands of the Hindus. To the Muslim an industrialized India meant a Hindu India. Finally, there was the political issue. The Muslim had memories of empire and fears of servitude; the Hindu had the reverse. To the Muslim, Hindu rule meant Hinduization, or the break up of all that he held dear and the degradation of his most cherished values. It was therefore not surprising that when the Hindu stretched out his hand for the sceptre the Muslim cried out for Pakistan.

6

Historical Perspective

THE EARLIEST CIVILIZATION KNOWN IN INDIA is that of the Indus valley. In the past forty years archaeologists have unearthed a city culture which has all the marks of being pre-Aryan and shows affinities to the early Sumerian culture of Iraq. The excavations of Sir John Marshall, Ernest Mackay, Sir Mortimer Wheeler, and others at Mohenjo-Daro, Chauho-Daro in Sind, and Harappa in the Punjab, have revealed cities with a high degree of development, with a modern drainage system, and kiln-baked bricks on the outer walls as evidence of a moister climate than the present. The intriguing and artistic seals which have been discovered have also been identified at Tel el Asmar in Iraq, thus suggesting at least a trade connexion. Writing was known though the script has not yet been deciphered. Clay and bronze figures suggest a considerable development of art, and children's toys indicate an advanced state of agricultural society where the wheel was already known. Wheat of a variety still found in the Punjab was cultivated. There is little sign so far of temples, but ritual objects found suggest a cult akin to that of Siva and the worship of the mother goddess common in the Middle East and also in South India. Lack of evidence makes it difficult to identify the Indus race, and the few human remains so far found provide doubtful and conflicting testimony. Nor do the few human figures help us. The stone head of a man with receding brow and thick protruding lips, is anything but Aryan.

Whence these people came, who they were, and whither they went is at present unknown. Successive strata of remains disappearing at last beneath the level of the subsoil water suggest a period of prosperity from about 2500 B.C. to 1500 B.C., with a stretch still earlier for origins and growth, since the lowest levels already show a fully-developed culture. The latter end of the people is the most intriguing mystery of all. Until recently the time gap between their disappearance and the date usually assigned to the coming of the Aryans (1500 B.C.) seemed too big to warrant a connexion, and the apparent lack of fortification did not accord with early Aryan stories of storming fortresses. At the same time the resemblance of the Indus cults to Hindu fertility cults and particularly the worship of Siva and his bull pointed in the opposite direction. But the most recent investigations at Harappa have revealed extensive fortifications, together with traces of fire. It thus seems that the time vacuum which historians abhor may be filled and the Aryans revealed as the conquerors of the Indus people and borrowers of their culture. The Indus people were a copper-using folk ignorant of iron, and this fact would provide good reason for Aryan success.

The extent of the Indus culture is not yet fully known. It obviously flourished in Sind, Baluchistan, and the Central Punjab; remains have been found as far west as Rupar, where the Sutlej emerges from the hills. There is no present physical obstacle to its extension right down to the Bay of Bengal; an aerial survey may before long enable this point to be settled. If, however, as the evidence so far suggests, Sind and the Punjab enjoyed a larger rainfall than at present, the Ganges valley may have been too swampy and forest-logged to be suitable for a highly developed city culture. Experience elsewhere shows that early civilizations tended to develop in dry but fertile regions rather than in damp climates, where nature was too formidable an obstacle.

History, though not recorded history, begins with the coming of the Aryans, and it is here, in the absence of any certain knowledge of the relation of the Indus culture to the rest of Indian history, that our historical perspective really begins. It is common to refer to Indian history as a series of invasions. Tribes broke in, conquered and settled, and were then overcome in their turn, right down to the advent of the British. *Veni, vidi, vici, victus sum*, is the current mental picture of Indian history. But this is an over-simplification. In the first place there was more than one kind of conquest, and in the second the movements were not always in the same direction.

Invasions of India have been of two main kinds. Setting aside mere raids, like those of the famous Mahmud of Ghazni in the eleventh century, the terrible Taimur in the fourteenth, and the Persians and Afghans in the eighteenth, they have been either folk movements or military conquests. Folk movements may replace one people by another, as the Anglo-Saxons replaced the Britons in the eastern half of England, or mix one people with another, as the same Anglo-Saxons mixed with the Britons in the west, or the Franks with the Gallo-Romans of fifth-century Gaul, or superimpose one people on another, as the Vandals did in North Africa and the modern Anglo-Dutch have done in South Africa. If the conquered are too numerous to be exterminated, or too tenacious to be enslaved or permanently subordinated, they may absorb their conquerors as did the Chinese with the Mongols and the Manchus. Indian history begins with a folk movement which subordinated the conquered without exterminating them or being absorbed by them; it continues with a series of absorptions, more or less speedy, more or less complete; and ends with a movement which conquered but neither exterminated nor enslaved nor was absorbed, and which in consequence today forms an indigestible morsel in the Hindu body cultural. This last movement is that of the Muslims.

Folk movements depend for their effectiveness on their standard of culture. If their standard is lower than those they conquer they are easily assimilated and only the physical effect remains. If higher, they may effect a real revolution and start history anew. If the standard of invader and conquered is both high, they may mingle and influence each other, or may remain apart and produce a permanent fissure in the social structure. The former happened to the Aryans and the latter with the Muslims.

Military conquests can produce little physical effect because of limitation of numbers, but they may, if the conquerors are advanced in cultural ideas and suitably recruited, produce important political and social changes. This is what has happened in the case of the British. Otherwise conquests are not historically significant, for there is nothing so transitory as pure military action. The sword can cut but not mould; you can, as has been said, do anything with bayonets except sit on them. With these considerations in mind, we can return to the early Aryans.

The advent of the Aryans is usually dated at about 1500 B.C. The only thing known for certain about them is that they came from the north-west. Linguistic and literary evidence suggests that they were part of a great complex of folk movements which brought the ancient Persians into Persia, the Greeks into the Aegean basin, and the Latins into Italy. The Mitanni, a tribe in contact with the Hittites in 1400 B.C., had gods identifiable with those of the Indo-Aryans; Sanskrit has close affinities with Avestic, Greek, and Latin, and all these peoples had common characteristics, such as fair skins, the use of iron, the burning of their dead, flowing clothes, and the triple institution of king, council, and assembly. The Aryans worshipped the powers of nature, like Indra the storm god and Usha the dawn, and it is from their noble hymns to these deities (now forming the *Rig-Veda*) that we learn something of their life and institutions and know that their first centre was Afghanistan and the Punjab. They were a pastoral and agricultural people, counting their wealth in cattle, organized on patriarchal lines, attaining high skill in handicrafts, trading by means of barter, and fond of hunting and the chase. 'War begat the king' in Vedic as in Teutonic history generally, but the king was aided and restrained by a council of nobles and the general assembly of the people. They had an aversion to the dark-skinned aboriginals and celebrated their triumphs against them. With the passage of the centuries the scene shifted eastward; society grew more complex and thought probed deeper. The region of the Jumna and upper Ganges became the homeland or Aryavarta of the people whose epic sites can still be identified. Contact with the still despised aboriginals developed the caste system. The literature of ritual, worship, and speculation grew rapidly until it flowered in the philosophical *Upanishads* which are the basis of all later Hindu thought. With these came the doctrines of illusion (*maya*), moral consequences (*karma*), transmigration, and spiritual freedom. Vishnu and Siva emerged as major deities. The old nature gods fell into the background and Hinduism achieved recognizable shape and character. Politically separate kingdoms appeared and it is possible to draw the first political and sociological map of India.

These developments occupied some thousand years until the eve of the historical period. The central Hindu strand of Indian life had been woven. But before Indian history became a tale of invasions, others had to be added. The sixth century B.C. was an age of intellectual unrest in India, rather like the parallel period in Greece and the Augustan age in the Mediterranean world. Men were increasingly dissatisfied with pure ritual as a key to life and not willing to take Brahmin abstractions in substitution. The contrast between social customs backed by Brahminical authority and the moral sense weighed heavily, and men looked for a way of renewal or escape which was something more than a mental exercise. Two of the many sects of this period have survived, one within and one without India. The first and lesser is Jainism whose founder, Mahavira, lived in north India about 540–468 B.C., and the second and greater is Buddhism whose founder, Siddhartha Gautama, the Buddha or en-lightened one, probably lived from about 560 to 480 B.C. Jainism taught that each soul was eternally distinct and separate, bound to unending rebirths until right knowledge was attained. The path of release was asceticism and the scrupulous respect of all sentient beings. Jainism is a sect today less than two million strong, but it has deeply influenced the general Hindu body. It perhaps is more responsible than anything else for the streak of *ahimsa* or non-violence in Hindu thought and practice.

Buddhism, like Jainism, began both as an attempt to provide a satisfying explanation of and antidote to the evil of life and as a protest against the sacerdotal authority of the Brahmins. It was both a moral and intellectual movement, preaching moral reform and intellectual enlightenment simultaneously. The Buddha began by announcing that desire was the secret of sorrow and suffering, the cord that bound men to the wheel of life. Agnostic about ultimate reality, he provided with his noble eightfold path and four virtues a way of salvation for the householder as well as the ascetic. The world was evil, but a way of escape was open, a way consisting of right action and right thought. Life did not consist of ritual actions, but of working out one's salvation energetically. Buddha provided a moral code and way of life for his followers, and a community or church to bind them together. Though he only thought of himself as the discoverer of the impersonal truth about the universe, he gave concrete form to the universal religion implicit in Hinduism. Buddhism developed from a negative spiritual discipline to a world religion with the Buddha himself, that sublimely assured sceptic, as the saviour god of an eastern evangelicalism. Because of its clear-cut creed and emphasis on brotherhood, Buddhism cut across caste and Brahminical claims, and because of its severe moral code it clashed with the Brahmin countenance of moral abuses like polygamy. It was in fact the Protestant Reformation of the Eastern world. The life and precepts of its founder have a strong fascination for a Western world dominated by action and drugged by materialism and dimly suspicious that these after all may not be the infallible way of salvation. The organization of the Buddhist church, its theology, ritual, monastic life, and hagiology, all suggest a kind of inverted gospel—the negative pole of positive Christianity. To the Gospel injunction, 'If any man thirst, let him come unto me and drink,' the Buddha replies, 'Whom thirst conquers, thirst the contemptible, for him shall sorrow multiply as the grass grows; who conquers thirst, thirst the contemptible, which is hard to escape from in this world, for him will suffering fall away like the water drops from the lotus flower.'

The rise and spread of Buddhism is a fascinating subject, and its disappearance from India one of the great historical mysteries. For our purposes it is only possible to consider its significance in the development of India as a whole. That is both external and internal. Organized Buddhism existed abroad in its earlier form (the Hinayana or lesser vehicle) in Ceylon, Burma, and Siam, and as a theistic universal church in its later form (the Mahayana or greater vehicle) in China, Japan, and, with further modifications, in Tibet. Carried by missionaries across the sea to Burma and Siam, and via Afghanistan and central Asia to China, Buddhism has been the principal vehicle for the export of Indian culture, and through it Indian religious, social, and artistic influence has spread throughout the Far East. One of the greatest Indian cultural monuments is the Buddhist *stupa* of Borobudur in Java. Indian art-forms are to be found in the ruins of the desiccated cities of central Asia discovered by Sir Aurel Stein and have markedly influenced Chinese art. They have penetrated all through Indonesia, though not always here in their Buddhist form.

Internally, the influence of Buddhism is not to be judged from its visible traces. It is true that Buddha has been absorbed into the Hindu sponge by recognition as the ninth incarnation of Vishnu, but in popular religion Buddha as a personality counts for very little. The real proof of his influence is a comparison of the Hinduism which succeeded Buddhism with that which preceded it. For though the system was fundamentally the same, the Hinduism of the sixth century B.C. was a very different thing from the Hinduism of the twelfth century A.D. The great failure of Buddhism was its inability to break up caste, its great success its ability to reform Hinduism. It must be remembered that there never was a time when Buddhism ousted Hinduism altogether. They always existed side by side, reacting on each other and rising and falling with alternations of court favour. Buddhism's first great triumph was the patronage of the Emperor Asoka (*c.* 274–237 B.C.) who made it the state religion and adopted that novel form of propaganda, the erection of pillars inscribed with Buddhist precepts and the carving of rock inscriptions. Its death-blow was the overthrow of the Buddhist Palas of Bengal by the Sen kings in the tenth century A.D. The new Brahminism was modified morally by the abandonment of Brahmin polygamy and the vicarious begetting of heirs, socially by the adoption of vegetarianism, and ceremonially by the virtual abandonment of animal sacrifice. Intellectually, Hindu philosophy developed a highly polished theism and the grammarian Panini promoted an exactitude of expression and a precision of terminology which made Sanskrit a far more precise vehicle for human thought than Pali or, indeed, most other languages. Controversy gave birth to Hindu logic and by its means custom was modified and turned into that monument of ingenuity, Hindu law. The Buddhists, it has been said, were out-argued, out-worshipped, and out-manoeuvred in daily life. Finally, Buddhism left in its monastic paintings, whose masterpiece is at Ajanta, a priceless legacy of art which has been the inspiration of the modern Indian art revival. For all its apparent disappearance, Buddhism lives on in some of the most impressive features of historical Hinduism.

We now return to the invasions of India. The first and most famous of these is the incursion of Alexander in 326 B.C. This was more than a raid for Alexander founded cities and established governors, and though within twenty years Greek rule gave place in the Punjab and Afghanistan to the Indian empire of Chandragupta, the Greek kingdom of Bactria maintained a flow of Hellenic influence. For a time Indo-Greek kingdoms controlled the north-west from Taxila, and we know their rulers and dynasties from their coins. This interlude proved invaluable to the historian for a knowledge of India which the inquisitive Greeks passed on to the West, but it also had its influence on India itself. The Greeks readily adopted Indian cults which they equated with their own, but they equally eagerly introduced Greek art and architecture. The Buddhist Gandhara school of sculpture and architectural remains in Taxila and Kashmir bears witness to this activity. Perhaps most important of all was the imperial tradition. Before Alexander's time there were no Indian empires; the first Mauryan empire was stimulated by opposition to the Seleucid successors of Alexander. The Achaemenid Persians provided a model and their Greek successors the necessary stimulus. Persian influence can be traced in Mauryan imperial institutions and Persian art-forms found their way into Indian architecture (for example the lion capitals of Asokan pillars).

For more than a thousand years after the time of Alexander the history of northern India is an alternation of migratory invasions with spacious interludes of Indian imperial rule. Unlike the Greeks, the invaders were lower in the scale of culture than the Indians and were consequently subject to the law of absorption. There was physical but not ideological or social change. A rhythm can be traced of destructive conquest, settlement, assimilation, and imperial rule. There were the Parthians, the Sakas and Kushans, the latter a branch of the central Asian Mongolian Yueh-Chi. They embraced Buddhism and dominated the north-west and Afghanistan from the first to the third centuries A.D. The rise of the Sassanian Persian empire then barred barbarian incursions, and Indian imperialism reasserted itself in the long-lived Gupta empire, the Indian counterpart of the Age of the Antonines. In the fifth century A.D. came a fresh wave of invasions. The Gujaras settled, gave their name to Gujarat, and left their mark in the Gujar community of northern India. The Hunas, or White

Huns, devastated the Punjab and destroyed its flourishing Buddhist civilization along with the great university city of Taxila. This was perhaps the greatest single blow which Indian civilization has ever suffered. In this barbarian flood old landmarks disappeared and peoples were uprooted. This is the real dividing line between ancient and medieval India. But the Hindu sponge absorbed this flood also, and out of the confusion rose the Rajputs and the sturdy Jat community. The brief imperial interlude of Harsha in the seventh century ushered in the long era of Rajput chivalry which lasted till the rise of Islam in India.

The origin of the Rajputs is not precisely known; all that can be said with certainty is that before the troubles of the fifth century there were few traces of them, and that in the seventh century they emerge upon the stage of Indian history fully armed, like Minerva, for the age of Indian chivalry. During the next five centuries there were few great empires and few great imperial organizations. No definite reason can be assigned, though we can make several conjectures. Possibly the balance of power was too even to be upset. Another factor was the absence of further stimulus from outside, either by way of invasion or imperial model. There was no challenge to evoke an imperial response. The clan spirit of the new Rajput tribes must also have worked against unity, as it has continued to do ever since. These tribes had no imperial tradition themselves and broke up the Hindu Gupta empire too thoroughly for the Indian tradition to survive. Their allegiance was given to the Hindu system itself and not to Hindu imperialism—the reverse process to that of the Teutons in the West, who rejected the Roman social system but held the imperial name and structure in awe. While the first five centuries saw the flowering of Sanskrit literature and drama, personified by the poets Kalidasa and Valmiki, and the development of the great epic poems of the Mahabharata (Great War) and Ramayana (story of Rama), the Rajput period saw the development of classical Hindu architecture and of romantic bardic poetry. The ballads of Hindu chivalry, still popular with the people of the north, date from this period.

Throughout this period Buddhism declined at the expense of Brahminism until it survived only as a popular and hardly recognizable cult in Bengal. There was little sign of internal development. The period was one of political confusion and cultural stiffening. A challenge was overdue and it came in the form of the Islamic religion and Turkish invaders. The first contact of Islam with India was the conquest of Sind by the Arab Mohammad bin Kasim in 712. But Sind, as has been explained, was a blind alley for Indian conquest, and the Muslims advanced no further for three centuries. At the end of the tenth century fresh tribal movements from central Asia brought the Turks into Afghanistan and into contact with Hinduism. Mahmud of Ghazni made a series of raids early in the eleventh century culminating in the sack of Somnath in Gujarat and of Mathura on the Jumna. The positive result was the conquest of most of the Punjab. But again there was a pause while the Rajputs continued their wars of honour and dynastic revolutions. The real invasion began at the end of the twelfth century when the Turkish chief Mohammad of Ghor defeated the Rajput hero Prithvi Raj and captured Delhi in 1192. A new age had begun.

The new invasion was primarily a military conquest, but since the invading armies were reinforced by a steady stream of adventurers from the north-west, who settled their families in the country, it had some of the effects of a migration as well. The settlement of the Turks in India was encouraged by the early cutting adrift of the Delhi rulers from the suzerainty of Ghor, as the loss of Normandy in 1204 anchored the Norman aristocracy to English soil. This separation was soon after confirmed by the ravages in Persia of Chinghiz Khan and his wild Mongols. Thus the Turkish invaders became a military aristocracy spread thinly over the country and preserved by the Hindu inability to organize combined resistance for any length of time. The natural fate of the Turks —like the Huns, the Gujaras, the Sakas, and the Kushans—would have been assimilation to Hinduism. But in this case the sponge failed to work; the object to be absorbed was too solid. The Turks were kept together at first by discipline, tribal ties, and a sense of common danger, but what preserved them in the long run was the Muslim religion fortified by Persian culture. Islam gave them something to fight and die for, and that feeling of moral superiority which is the best antidote against the insidious germ of inferiority which is the beginning of cultural paralysis. Persian culture gave them intellectual self-respect and so to speak completed their cultural armour. So the usual order of events was reversed, and it was Islam which made inroads upon Hinduism. A few high-caste Hindus came in from conviction or policy, others from awe or terror. But amongst the lowest or outcaste Hindus there was something of a spontaneous movement, which attained its largest proportions in Bengal, where it captured half the population. This, as has already been mentioned, was possibly due to the undertone of Buddhist discontent with an unsympathetic Hindu monarchy.

The Delhi Sultanate was the centre of Muslim power for two centuries and restores some unity to Indian history. At first Delhi was the headquarters of the Turkish army in India, and then it became the capital of a military kingdom something like, on a much larger scale, the crusading kingdom of Jerusalem in the twelfth century. But if there was no assimilation of Muslims to Hindus, there was a gradual development of mutual toleration (with interludes of persecution) and of a workable *modus vivendi*. Hindus were freely employed and came to dominate the revenue and financial services. Hindu philosophy exercised its spell on Muslim scholars, as is shown in the work of the greatest of them, Alberuni. The result was seen in the eclecticism of the Muslim Sufi movement in India and the passionate poems of the fifteenth-century Kabir. The oil and water did not combine, but they interspersed on the fringes and developed curious eddies within themselves.

Politically the Delhi Sultanate performed a dual function. It fought the Hindus in the centre and south until for a few brief years (1311–34) Delhi controlled almost the whole of India except the deeper fastnesses of Rajputana and the extreme south. Thenceforward the Deccan was ruled by a series of Muslim succession kingdoms, while south of the Kistna Hinduism at last developed a political antibody to the Muslim virus and emerged as the empire of Vijayanagar, the wonder of the first Portuguese observers in India. Externally the Sultans acted as the wardens of the marches against the Mongol flood which devastated Persia and Iraq in the thirteenth century. When the next invasion wrecked the Delhi empire in 1398, its leader was the Turkish Taimur or Tamerlane. Taimur's invasion turned out to be a mere military raid, though a bloody one. Taimur turned to China and died on its marches and India was left alone for more than a century. Politically the damage was only slowly repaired, but culturally the period saw an outburst of exquisite art, which, released from the constricting centralism of Delhi, adorned provincial capitals with a wealth of local styles. As soon as the Mongol menace was removed, migration from the north continued steadily and to this modern India owes a large proportion of the more vigorous section of the Muslim community.

The Muslim era in India reached its peak with the Moghul empire. Its founder Babur, most delightful of autobiographists, was a direct descendant of the Turkish Taimur, but so completely imbued with Persian culture that there was no serious cultural clash between Moghul and Indian Muslim. His advent was rather a stimulus to progress along lines already marked out. He and his Moghuls had something of the same vivifying effect upon Muslim Indian policy as William the Conqueror and his Normans had on Saxon England. There was a new vigour, a new unity, a new constructive purpose leading on to a new synthesis. As with the contemporary Elizabethan period, so with the reign of Akbar, it seemed for a time that the world's great age was beginning anew. Not a little of this was due to the genius of the ruling family which, through seven generations, maintained a standard bordering on or passing into brilliance; it is significant that as soon as the family genius deserted the emperors the stately fabric collapsed. Culturally the Muslims reached the highest pitch of their excellence. The Taj Mahal and the Jama Masjid of Delhi and the palaces of Agra and Fatehpur Sikri crowned their architectural endeavour; the Moghul school of painting in miniature revealed the delicacy of their artistic sensibility; the encyclopedic learning of Abul Fazl rivalled that of Alberuni, and the quatrains of his poet brother Faizi the Persian masters; the Moghul court, like Versailles in Europe, became a school of manners for the whole sub-continent. The administrative arrangements were used by the British as the foundation of their own. A fresh approach to Hindu-Muslim understanding was shown both in such movements as the Sikh cult of Guru Nanak (in its earlier stages) and the 'Divine Faith' of Akbar himself, and the graceful intermingling of Hindu and Muslim art-forms in the new Moghul style. A significant sign of greatness was the welcome accorded to foreigners of every kind from Portuguese Jesuits to French jewellers, and the interest shown not only in foreign novelties like watches and mechanical toys, but in ideas as well. Akbar delighted in Jesuit discussions of their faith and Dara Shikoh ordered translations both of the Gospels and of the Upanishads.

The political history of the Moghul empire followed the general pattern, with certain noteworthy features. After early years of struggle Akbar consolidated an imperial realm as far as the Indian Ocean, the river Narbada, and the central India jungles. Thereafter his successors steadily extended their dominion until Aurangzeb, in the late seventeenth century, controlled practically the whole of India. Akbar rested his dominion on an understanding with the Hindus in general and the Rajputs in particular which amounted to a partnership in the empire. Hindus were amongst his trusted councillors, Rajput rajahs governed provinces and commanded armies. A politico-military service brought the motive of honour to the service of the crown and united the communities in a joint membership. His synthetic religion was a failure, but the result of Akbar's work was the establishment of a truly Indian empire under Muslim leadership, which Hindus could accept without reserve. Shah Jahan was the Kublai Khan or Haroun-al-Raschid of the Moghul empire, the stately president of a régime in the full tide of wealth and prosperity. It was the reports of the empire at this period by the Portuguese Jesuits, the English ambassador Roe, and the French doctor Bernier which so impressed seventeenth-century Europe with Indian wealth and splendour. With Aurangzeb (1658–1707) decline began. The rising hope of the 'high' Muslim party, he began by displacing his 'broad' Muslim brother Dara Shikoh in civil war. By actions comparable to Louis XIV's revocation of the Edict of Nantes he lost the sympathy of the Hindu masses and the active support of most of the Rajput rajahs. He attacked the southern Muslim kingdoms and at the same time provoked a rebellion of the 'mountain rats' of western India, the skinny but wiry Marathas, under their redoubtable leader Sivaji. The Marathas pierced the Moghul Achilles' heel. With wonderful tenacity Aurangzeb persevered unflinchingly until his death at the age of eighty-eight without completing their subjugation. He left the whole empire in such a state of tension, political, religious, and economic, that it would have required an Akbar to restore the situation. But no Akbar was forthcoming. Instead there followed Bahadur Shah, 'the Heedless', and Mohammad Shah, 'the Jolly' or 'Pleasure-Loving'. The Moghul genius had departed. Delhi was sacked by Nadir Shah the Persian in 1739 and by the Afghans in 1756 and 1760, and from that time ceased to exist as a political entity. Only dignity and courage redeemed the impotence of the last active emperor, Shah Alam, who, when tauntingly asked by his torturer whether he could see at the moment of being blinded, replied, 'Nought but the Koran between me and thee.' He composed on the occasion one of the most moving odes of Indo-Persian literature.

During the Moghul period India enjoyed a degree of prosperity greater perhaps than that of any age since that of the Guptas. This was largely because on the whole she enjoyed greater security, so that a higher proportion of the national income could be spent on productive and capital works (including architectural monuments) rather than on armies and fortresses. The world beyond her borders both east and west was also in a non-aggressive and prosperous condition. Internal prosperity made trade profitable and external conditions stimulated demand. It was the profits of a flourishing trade, together with the surplus of land revenue returns over administrative and military expenses, which enabled the Moghuls to maintain their sumptuous courts and to erect their magnificent buildings. Much of their expenditure was, in the strict economic sense, quite unproductive, but it was this which so impressed European observers with the boundless wealth of India. It is probably true to say that the *per capita* income in India under Akbar compared favourably with that of England, while surplus wealth at the disposal of the government was probably greater. From 1650 onwards, however, the commercial and productive development in Europe was balanced by no corresponding advance in India, and it was from this time that India began relatively to fall behind in the economic race.

Europe was directly dependent on India for spices and drugs. Spices were a necessity to salt or 'powder' meat for winter use, since cattle had to be killed in the autumn owing to lack of fodder. They were also used to season meat highly, a custom prevalent in England until the reign of Charles II. This again was not pure luxury, but often necessary to conceal the taste of tainted or ill-preserved meat. The major spices it is true came from the East Indies, but it was India through which they had to pass. In Roman times there was a direct trade from the Malabar coast through Egypt, taking advantage of the monsoon winds. The Romans were succeeded by the Arabs, and Europe thus found that it had to pay two sets of middlemen instead of one. The Crusades were directed to Egypt partly for this reason and their failure made things more difficult. What Europe needed enriched the infidel, and this gave a double motive for seeking the sea passage to India—securing the necessary spices direct and ruining the Egyptians by cutting off both spices and profits. The fact that the Egyptian trade was monopolized by the Venetians gave the Genoese a good reason for backing the Portuguese in their African explorations.

Vasco da Gama reached Calicut in South India in 1497, nearly thirty years before Babur reached Delhi. The Portuguese at once set out to to control the all-important spice trade for themselves, and under Albuquerque established a maritime empire with stations ranging from Malacca in the East Indies to the Persian Gulf and the East African coast. Their passion for quick profits caused them to concentrate on the spice trade, their cruelty and perfidy aroused Indian hostility, and their early loss of vigour prevented them from ever controlling much territory beyond the range of the guns of their ships and fortresses.

Monopoly is the mother of jealousy, and it was inevitable that their control of the Indian trade should be challenged by other powers as soon as conditions permitted. In 1580 Portugal passed under the control of Philip II's Spain, and so became fair game for his enemies. The defeat of the Armada in 1588 and the subsequent Spanish naval decline gave the Protestant powers their chance, and within a few years Dutch and English ships found their way to the East. Both had their eye on the spice trade, and so both at first regarded India as a secondary theatre. Because of their small bulk, spices were easily carried even by the small ships of those days and the profits were enormous, so there was much to be gained by going straight to the source of supply. So the Europeans in India during the sixteenth and seventeenth centuries were an added element to the variety of Indian life, but neither a dominant factor nor a political danger. Individual adventurers found their way to India in increasing numbers, to trade like the jeweller Tavernier, practise their professions like the French doctor Bernier, or to serve the Moghul government as artillerymen or ordinary soldiers. Their accounts are most valuable sources of knowledge for conditions in India, but their influence in sum was small. The gorgeous East was unveiled, but a new turn of events was necessary to convert individual and commercial contact into conquest or control and to take the gorgeous East in fee.

7
The British

IT IS A TRUISM that the British went to India as traders, and it is often added that their empire accrued in a fit of absence of mind. But it would be more accurate to say that the British acquired India behind the backs of the Directors of the East India Company and largely against their wishes. The Company preferred profit to conquest, but directorial disapproval of annexation rarely ran to reversal so long as the profits came in. What the Company would not sow it was not always ashamed to reap. The Company's hands were frequently forced by their servants, and, in the English way, they finally came to be proud of it.

It is beyond the scope of this book to narrate the history of the British in India. We are only concerned here to note the significance of the British in India, both in what they brought to the country and what they did there. They were not the only or the fundamental factor at work in modern India, but they were certainly an important element, and a glance at the circumstances of their rise helps in the understanding of their behaviour when once they had achieved dominion. The subject can be approached by way of answers to the questions: Why was it the British who became the principal European traders in India? Why and how did the merchants convert their counting-houses into council chambers, their broadcloth into uniform? And, having done so, how came they to control a whole sub-continent many times as large as their own country? Finally, what did they do with supreme power once they had achieved it?

The answer to the first question is that the English were too much for the Portuguese, but not strong enough to stand up to the Dutch in the East Indies. The Portuguese, who controlled both the spice trade and the traffic of the Indian Ocean, opposed both powers, but, with the defeat of their fleet in 1615 off Surat, pass out of the story. The Dutch made first for the East Indies and ousted the Portuguese and then developed a chain of stations via Ceylon, South India, and the Cape to connect them with the Netherlands. The English followed, but in Dutch eyes a common faith did not mean sharing profits. The English were ejected from the East Indies, and owing to the Civil War and later conflicts never obtained redress. Thus excluded from the spice trade at its source, they concentrated on the less lucrative Indian traffic, which was largely in cotton piecegoods. This trade attracted them to the north and so brought them into contact with the Moghul empire. The Portuguese had relied on the spice trade for their main wealth; their activity in the north was subsidiary and mainly a commercial stranglehold of the sea-going traffic from India to the Middle East. The moment the Moghuls realized that the English could give security from the Portuguese at sea, both for commerce and pilgrims, they made them privileged traders. The British became the Moghul Government's naval auxiliaries.

Thus began a century of quiet trading. The merchants lived within 'factories' or collegiate merchant settlements, where a common life was observed, including a dinner in Hall, prayers morning and evening, and a curfew at night. When not engaged on the Company's investment the merchants prosecuted their private ventures in India or overseas in the East Indies, by which they hoped to get rich and return home for good. Often they married Portuguese or Indian women locally and settled down to semi-Indianized lives. They loved feasts and drinking bouts (like Muslim nobles) in the Company's gardens; their ears became attuned to the country music and their eyes to the country dancing girls; they loved processions, the beating of drums, and the firing of cannon. But consistent recruitment prevented denationalization, and careful and sometimes grandmotherly supervision too much corruption.

The next question is how sober traders became soldiers and politicians. As the Moghul authority declined factories became fortified settlements, but this change was brought about to safeguard trading operations, not to form bases for aggression. Delhi had fallen to Persian attack before the British entered Indian politics seriously. The growing weakness of the Moghul régime had another effect. Not only the foreign invader but also the internal careerist appeared. Provinces became petty kingdoms and rebels potentates. Thus the Maratha power grew in the west, Hyderabad split off in the south, and Bengal in the east. The new rulers had their careerists in their turn, and so the whole country was gradually reduced to a condition of confusion and conflict, the moment of succession being the signal for interference. Given this situation we have only to add an energetic European nation to precipitate a period of conflict, and this the French with their enterprise and polish, their imagination and ambition, provided. There was no need to wait for successions; Europe from 1740 provided the wars which justified French merchant and British factor in seizing sword and musket, drilling Indian troops, and fighting either directly or as auxiliaries to Indian princes. As soon as their struggle began, something became obvious which had long been suspected. Since Babur had won Panipat with the help of Turkish artillerymen, European military science as well as European wealth had forged far ahead of current Indian practice. There was a triple difference of discipline, of arms, and of morale. The small standing army maintained by the early Moghuls had long disappeared and there was nothing on the Indian side to match the European tradition of discipline which already went back two hundred years to the Spanish infantry of the sixteenth century. Arms, especially artillery and muskets, were similarly superior; the competitive European world had proved a hothouse of development. And there was an even greater difference in morale. The Europeans in a sense were all adventurers, fighting with their backs to the sea, having everything to gain and little to lose. Their Indian opponents were all men involved in the elaborate net of Indian politics; they were mercenaries, but not last-ditch adventurers, seeking fortune for which it was necessary to live to fight another day, and always hopeful, in the confused conditions of the times, of a turn in fortune's wheel. They were emphatically not fighting to the death; changing sides, bargains, and compromises were as common as in fifteenth-century Italy. Even private soldiers had to be careful, for their horses were their fortune and private property not easily replaced if injured in battle. Thus it came about that the Europeans acquired both moral and material ascendancy in Indian politics, and the addition of a handful of European troops on one side might mean the ruin of thousands of equally brave Indian soldiers on the other. Here was a challenge to which contemporary India had no reply.

The French started the process by backing a pretender to the throne of Hyderabad and seizing virtual control of that state; the British retaliated by promoting the rebellion of their own local ruler from Hyderabad and then controlling him. In the same way the British control of Bengal resulted from an opening move in the eastern phase of the Seven Years' War between France and England. France lost her hold in India essentially through lack of sea-power; her brilliant diplomacy could not be backed up by adequate forces because her troops could not be sustained by sufficient reinforcements. British dominion in India was a by-product of an Anglo-French struggle for commercial monopoly.

The acquisition of Bengal by Clive transformed the position of the British in India on account of its wealth and its strategic position. Bengal resources enabled the British to develop a disciplined Indian army, to stop the mouths of cavilling critics in London, and to enrich themselves at the same time. It is hardly surprising that such a dazzling prospect should have so turned the heads of these merchant soldiers that the Company was threatened with bankruptcy in 1772. The home government was thus provided with its first occasion for interference. The British were henceforth one of the great Indian powers, but not yet the sole Indian power. There was a British dominion in India but not of India.

The step from parity to primacy took just sixty years. It was marked by a series of campaigns, each one in general more arduous than the last. The campaigns against Tipu Sultan or the Maratha chiefs were of a very different order from the cannonade of Plassey. This was partly because the Indian princes realized that what was at stake was not their existence as individuals, but as a whole order; not which relative should rule a state, but which should rule India. Therefore they fought with increasing resolution, and at last, when too late, with desperation. It was also because India was beginning to develop the first antidotes to the foreign virus in the shape of the adoption of European methods of warfare. Each prince in turn formed disciplined battalions and parks of artillery. They were undone, not by inefficiency or by bad leadership, for neither of these was an Indian monopoly, but by the dwindling resources of the Indian economy. Western methods were expensive; India was already exhausted by decades of war which, by devastating the countryside, cut off at its source the revenue which was needed to pay the disciplined troops. Lack of pay meant reliance on loot, and loot meant the flight of the cultivator and no revenue. In the later eighteenth century the movements of armies were often determined, not by strategy, but by the need of ready money to pay the troops. The process would have taken longer, and might even have been arrested altogether, but for the fact that the moment of British expansion coincided with that of Indian political disintegration. The Moghul empire had already dissolved as a power, though not as a legal system, when the British established their control of Bengal. The natural successors of the Moghuls were the Marathas, but at the very moment of the British appearance in Bengal they met in violent collision invading Afghans from the north. The decisive battle of Panipat in 1761 was really a defeat for both Afghans and Marathas, for the former retreated to their mountains, while the latter received a shock which began the dissolution of their own confederacy into five suspicious and warring factions. The chance of a Maratha empire of India was gone, and the north from the Ganges to the Indus was given over to a generation of desolating political anarchy. A political vacuum was created which drew in the British, as the one stable power in India, as a magnet draws iron. The Anglo-Maratha wars were increasingly not wars against the Marathas as a whole, but against each section of them in turn. The final struggle was precipitated by British measures to round up the nests of plunderers called Pindaris which had grown up in Central India and whose ravages had extended to the British territories. Not all the territory which the British controlled was directly ruled; far from it. Much of it remained in the hands of Indian princes who accepted British suzerainty as the price of continued existence. The method with the larger was the introduction of subsidiary British forces stationed in the States and paid for by the princes, who thus bought security from more powerful princes at the price of sub-ordination to the British. It was, after all, only the traditional method of Indian imperialism more scientifically executed, and the princes' acceptance of an overruling power was the traditional method of preserving their existence in the face of a new dominant power. The difference was that the new power was unique in its resources, and that, to borrow the classical description of Luther, it had 'strange eyes and wonderful ideas in its head'. Thus the princely order of British India arose: some States, like those of the Rajputs, were dynasties with a thousand years of rule behind them, for whom the new empire was a passing interlude; some were fragments of the Moghul empire founded by dissident Moghul governors, like the Nizam of Hyderabad; and some were survivors of the Maratha Confederacy, like Holkar and Sindhia. Others were adventurers who had built up little states of their own in troubled times, and were recognized as legitimate rulers in order to facilitate the settling of the country. When the process had been virtually completed in fact, it was cemented by the development of the doctrine of paramountcy. The new British were but old Moghuls writ large.

By the end of 1818 the British controlled the whole of India east of the Sutlej. By 1757, as a result of Plassey and the Carnatic wars, they had become one of the great powers; by 1805, as a result of the Maratha wars, they had become the principal power in India; now they were the paramount power. There only remained the work of completion; this occupied the next forty years, and its course was largely determined by chance and by trial and error. The Government still professed to desire no further annexations, but it was now a desire caused by fear of budget deficits rather than concern for commercial dividends. With this quite genuine desire went, however, a fear of encroachment which now seems almost pathological in relation to the resources of the possible aggressors. Behind Sind, the Punjab, Afghanistan, and Persia, lay the lengthening shadow of Russia. Britain and Russia clashed in the Near East. It was natural for Russia to try to make the British flesh creep in India as an offset for Palmerstonian rebuffs in Turkey, and it was inevitable in the circumstances that British statesmen should read far more into Russian moves eastwards than the facts warranted. The fate of the border regions was decided by the exigencies of the diplomatic duel between London and St. Petersburg.

The regions still uncontrolled were the Punjab, now under the firm rule of the one-eyed Sikh chief, Ranjit Singh; Sind, a confederacy of five Amirs or chiefs who had formerly owed allegiance to the Afghans and had once acknowledged the Moghuls; and Baluchistan. Beyond these states lay Afghanistan, the scene of continued dynastic turbulence; and, beyond again, Persia, where the long decline of the Kajar dynasty had started. To protect Afghanistan from a fancied Russian threat the British were led into the disastrous enterprise of the first Afghan war. By this crude demonstration of the trial and error principle the ultimate British Indian frontier was fixed at the Khyber Pass. As a direct consequence of the Afghan war Sind was annexed in 1843. There remained the Punjab. Ranjit Singh had in 1810, with remarkable prescience, refrained from war with the Company and had built up a powerful military monarchy west of the Sutlej. But his state suffered from the cardinal weakness of basing a modern military machine on a purely agricultural economy. Even in the early nineteenth century this was impossible for long, and at that time the Punjab had no canals to fertilize its barren lands. To maintain the military caste the country was impoverished, with the result that the army became omnipotent. With the death of the leader in 1839 the chiefs turned against each other in a mad struggle for supremacy. A series of assassinations and palace revolutions culminated in the invasion of British India as a desperate means of relief.

Baluchistan was added to the Empire in the seventies as part of the second Russian scare which resulted in the second Afghan War. There remained only the eastern frontier where Burma was annexed. The first Burmese war was the result of Burmese misconceptions about the power of states beyond their borders—a case of mental isolation leading to physical aggression. The final annexation of Upper Burma in 1886 was influenced by the desire to checkmate possible French encroachment from Indo-China. The year before Upper Burma was annexed, the Indian Congress held its first meeting in Bombay. This modest event was the first overt sign of the new India whose evolution we have now to consider.

8

The Organization of Power

WE HAVE NOW TO ANSWER the last of the questions posed in the preceding chapter: How did the British exercise the power which they had acquired? At first they were too awed by the magnitude of their achievement to have any large ambitions. The leading Company officials contemplated their conquests with a mixture of astonishment and fear. Metcalfe was never tired of emphasizing the 'precariousness' of the British dominion; Elphinstone feared 'that the belief that our Indian Empire will not be long lived is reason and not prejudice'; 'in an empire like that of India,' wrote Malcolm, 'we are always in danger'. Munro, the fourth of the great Indian administrators, considered innovation 'the ruling vice of our government'. Never did conquerors set so gloomily about the task of organizing an empire. If foreign powers did not destroy the empire, thought these men, the native army might rise, and if the native army did not rise, the people might themselves so far develop that they would oust the British from control. This, to Elphinstone, was 'the most desirable death for us to die . . . but this seems at an immeasurable distance'. Metcalfe recognized this possibility as the result of improving measures, but considered that the measures should be taken nevertheless. If neither foreign invasion nor mutiny nor improvement brought an end to British rule then a revival of religious feeling certainly would. With these sentiments among the leading administrators, it is clear that the British brought with them no revolutionary spirit into the country. Their immediate object was to restore, to conserve, to continue, rather than to destroy, to innovate, or to revolutionize. They saw themselves as the successors of the Moghuls, sitting like them on a religious volcano, but unlike them, having no roots in the country and depending upon a mercenary army of doubtful allegiance. As with the Moghuls, their best friend was the inertia of Indian life, the principle of live and let live, and their most dangerous enemy religious fanaticism.

The first object of the British was the elementary one of restoring order, and their next to organize the collection of revenue. The years of disturbance had left bands of discharged soldiers and groups of uprooted peasants roaming the country, and these had first to be suppressed. The whole machinery of government had broken down and had to be reconstructed. In the Delhi territory revenue officers had to go out with regular infantry and guns, and were sometimes received with such 'briskness' by the sturdy villagers as 'temporarily to stagger them'. The city of Delhi was divided into wards by groups of neighbouring villages for the purpose of loot, and it was not safe to visit the ruins outside for fear of being shot at from behind walls by stray marauders. All the villages which had not moved into mosques or walled enclosures were protected by mud walls, and rash was the man who camped in the open at night. It was not safe to travel from Delhi to Agra without an escort. Several of the neighbouring territorial chiefs rejoiced in the title of Plunderer. The same conditions, in greater or less degree, obtained throughout India outside the older British possessions in Bengal and the south.

For their models the British had their own experience in Bengal and the south and the practice of the Moghul rulers before them. In these territories, also, the Moghul tradition was strong and they had in the end paid attention to it. British government in Bengal had begun in the name of a governor nominally dependent on the Moghul emperors, and when direct rule began it was by a direct grant from the fugitive emperor. Clive himself had received imperial grants and had meditated a march to Delhi to reseat the emperor on his throne. The first British experiment in direct rule had not been happy. There was the scandal of the Nawab of Arcot's debts, when the Company ruled the rich Carnatic territory as the creditor of the Nawab, and its servants in their private capacity bled the country with further advances and exactions. There was the period of plunder in Bengal, when Clive marvelled at his own moderation and a man might make a fortune in a few years, lose it in England, make a second and lose it a second time, and return to India for a third. The human result of this was the terrible Bengal famine of 1770, when the Company congratulated itself on a good revenue collection in spite of it. Warren Hastings put an end to the worst excesses, and Cornwallis laid the axe to the root of the tree of corruption, but neither of them understood the conditions and traditions of the people they were ruling, and both erred with the best of intentions. The net result was a chastened spirit of respect for the past in the more serious administrators and a determination to find out the facts of the situation before settling the form of government. 'Innovation has been so little guided by a knowledge of the people', wrote Munro ruefully, 'that, though made after what was thought to be mature discussion, it must appear to them as little more than the result of mere caprice.' The consciousness of British mistakes, and an increasing knowledge of an ordered past, united to turn the eyes of the British towards the Moghul model.

This, then, is the first key to the organization of the British government in India. There was an underlying continuity between the Moghul and British régimes. The parent stem was recognizably the same, and if to that stem the British grafted new shoots, with often strange and surprising results, they did not affect the underlying and original continuity.

This continuity is revealed in several ways. From 1803 the Emperor of Delhi was a British pensioner, but his name was still one to conjure with, and he was regarded throughout India as the fount of lawful authority. The British did not dare to challenge Indian sentiment by openly taking his place, but in a long series of cautious encroachments they claimed one prerogative after another. The final proclamation of Queen Victoria as Empress of India in 1876 was the delayed completion of the whole process. The Moghul influence can next be seen in the tradition of official magnificence. The Moghul empire was administered by an official nobility whose emoluments, from the time of Akbar, were enormous, and whose lavish expenditure helped to create the European myth of the boundless wealth of India. The Moghul *seigneur* (so long as he enjoyed the imperial favour) was something of a demigod, and the Company's servant was nothing loth to assume the divine afflatus. Periodic reductions steadily reduced this grandeur, but though the civil and military officers felt keenly the smarts of successive clippings, they nevertheless remained the best-paid service in the world. This is the secret of civilian complaints of a niggardly government and of both English and Indian criticism of an unnecessary extravagance and pomp.

The third trace of Moghul influence is to be found in the structure of the administration. The Secretariat was undeniably British, but the dignified hierarchy of officialdom was equally undeniably Moghul. Above all, the influence is to be seen in the local and district administration, in the methods of revenue collection and of dealing with the peasants. The influence of Raja Todar Mal, Akbar's revenue minister, lived on in the British land administration.

The primary task of the British was the re-establishment of order and the organization of law. First came the ending of the anarchy just described, the making of the country safe for the common man. This involved the suppression of the *dacoits* or robber bands who have always sprung to life in India (as brigands do in China) when the hand of authority has weakened. When conditions favoured these robber bands they became little states, which explains why many Indian states of that time were little more than robber bands. This work was well and truly done, having the whole-hearted support of the peaceful population. It is, perhaps, the one part of the British achievement which has never been seriously challenged. Freedom from rapine meant freedom for cultivation, and freedom of cultivation meant security for religious and family life which is the essence of Hinduism. Incidentally it also meant increase of population.

Order was restored by the military, but to maintain it the police were organized. The police have been undeniably efficient and equally undeniably unpopular. 'As for the Police,' wrote Lord William Bentinck in 1832, 'far from being a protection for the people, I cannot better illustrate the public feeling regarding it, than by the following fact, that nothing can exceed the popularity of a recent regulation, by which if a robbery has been committed, the police are *prevented* from making any inquiry into it, except upon the requisition of the persons robbed; that is to say, the shepherd is a more ravenous beast of prey than the wolf.' The stigmata of corruption and unnecessary brutality attached themselves to the police from the beginning and have not yet been shaken off. It would be unjust to say that India got the police she deserved; it would be nearer the mark to suggest that India got the police which the character of the times brought forth. The methods of the police were those current in Moghul times and inevitable in periods of grave disorders, and their continuance has been an anachronism rather than calculated policy. Corruption of those responsible for order was again no new thing; it was perhaps more rampant under the British because the police possessed unchallenged authority with consequent greater opportunities for extortion and less fear of defiance. The shortcomings of the police were the result of past tradition which they failed wholly to shake off, rather than of a deliberate lapse into barbarity. The credit item of the police account is the maintenance of order; the debit item the failure to make the common man their friend. It is for history to strike the balance.

The organization of law for the whole sub-continent was a vast and complicated task which called forth one of the major efforts of the British constructive genius. There was a chaos of competing civil jurisdictions to be sorted out, a criminal law to be revised and administered, and provision to be made for the commercial law made necessary by the new developments of trade and industry. Hindus and Muslims and often sections amongst them, as well as lesser communities, had each their own customs and written codes. Each of them was linked with religion, that formidable power-barrel near which the Company hesitated to light the most modest reforming match. The first instinct was to let the existing laws go on of themselves, and the second to introduce English law. But the existing laws needed authority to interpret and adjudicate between them, and the use of English law by the Supreme Court of Calcutta led to the execution of the luckless Nand Kumar for a crime regarded as venial in Hindu law. The existing criminal law contained provisions which made the judicial eyes even of the eighteenth century blink. The solution was along the familiar line of Moghul practice with British improvements. Moghul criminal law was Muslim law based on the Koran, which was applicable to both Hindus and Muslims. Cornwallis published in 1793 the first code, which was really Muslim law shorn of some of its medieval features such as the loss of limbs and the refusal to accept the testimony of an unbeliever against a Muslim, and garnished with British embellishments. Since Muslim barbarities were excised, and British barbarities not consonant with Muslim law were not introduced, the result was an advance in humanity and a law which compared favourably with current codes in Europe. But this was only a makeshift, and it was for the nineteenth century to complete the work thus begun. Macaulay as Law Member in 1834 inaugurated the systematic codification of criminal law, which was completed in 1860 with the passing into law of the Indian Penal Code. A series of Law Commissions extended this work up to 1882 and erected an impressive structure of public civil law.

The problem of personal law was solved by reorganizing the Hindu and Muslim systems for their respective members. Where difference of interpretation or rival schools of thought existed it has been for the Courts to decide. Progress in this sphere has therefore in the main been by judicial interpretation, sometimes helped by agreed legislation. The innovation here introduced by the British has been the notions of reason and equity. To both Hindu and Muslim the law was divine, to be interpreted, but not to be abridged. To the British the law was an instrument of justice, to be moulded and tempered to its purpose. The highest legal tribunal was the Judicial Committee of the Privy Council in England, which had

Hindu and Muslim members for dealing with Indian cases. Under its learned and cautious lead the Indian Courts have striven 'to clarify and render Indian law definite and certain'. Gaps have been filled up from English experience where necessary, local customs have been recognized where expedient, and old usages modified where they conflicted with the developing conscience of the age. Even with this care and circumspection it was sometimes necessary to undo by legislation what had been decided by the Courts. By such cautious and careful means a new public law, criminal and civil, was developed, and the old systems of private law clarified and modified to meet modern needs. The success of this work can be judged from the fact that for all the criticism of the police, no one has suggested the abolition of the British corpus of Indian law.

To administer this law a dignified judicial hierarchy developed, from magistrates' courts of first instance to High Courts at the provincial capitals, the Federal Court at New Delhi, and the Judicial Committee of the Privy Council in London. There were a number of interesting features about this judicial system. It was partly official and partly not; that is to say, a proportion of the judicial posts were reserved for members of the civil service who had elected for a judicial career, while the rest were appointed from the legal profession. The judiciary was thus a mixture of the British and French systems with a bias, except in the highest Courts, towards the French. On the other hand, the rule of law applied in India as in England. Officials were amenable to the ordinary Courts; there was no *droit administratif*. The combination of these two factors has produced much misunderstanding. In general it may be asserted that the rule of law was a real rule; there were frequent occasions when the Courts called hasty or arbitrary officials to order and enforced their will. On the other hand, the large official element in the judicial ranks imparted a certain fellow-feeling for the executive, and executive acts and points of view tended, specially in the lower Courts, to be viewed through slightly official-tinted spectacles. The last feature of the system worth remark is the union of executive and judicial functions in the person of the Collector or Deputy Commissioner (district officer) through the greater part of India. This was originally a measure of power designed to provide the collector of revenue with the means of enforcing, collection, but it also made him on occasion plaintiff and judge in the same suit, as English J.P.s were when country gentlemen sat on the bench to hear poaching cases. It has continued up to the present, partly on grounds of economy, and partly because it has not excited sufficient indignation in practice to provoke a change.

English legal administration has undoubtedly exercised a great influence upon modern Indian life. It has introduced the idea of regularity as opposed to chance or whim, of rule as opposed to anarchy and violence. But he would be a bold man who would say that the rule of law and its respect as the embodiment of justice were as firmly rooted in India as in England, except among a certain section of the intelligentsia. For the masses the law is still a distant thing, something so complicated that it cannot be understood and can only be operated through the medium of lawyers whose connexion with popular ideas of justice is far from obvious. The cumbrous procedure, the niceties of law, the methods of weighing evidence make the whole system obscure to the general public, and cause the Courts to be regarded as a great lottery where success comes to the chance possessor of a lucky ticket. What the legal system has established in the popular mind has been not so much the rule of law or justice, as the rule of rule.

From the protection of life and limb and the administration of justice we pass to the immemorial centre of Indian life, the village. The villages (there are 700,000 of them in all India today) are the basic expression of Indian social life. Charles Metcalfe thus described them in 1830:

The Village Communities are little Republics, having nearly everything they want within themselves, and almost independent of any foreign relations. They seem to last where nothing else lasts. Dynasty after dynasty tumbles down; revolution succeeds to revolution; Hindu, Pathan, Mughul, Mahratta, Sikh, English, are masters in turn; but the village communities remain the same. In times of trouble they arm and fortify themselves; a hostile army passes through the country; the Village Community collect their cattle within their walls, and let the army pass unprovoked; if plunder and devastation be directed against themselves and the force employed be irresistible, they flee to friendly villages at a distance, but when the storm has passed over they return and resume their occupation. If a country remains for a series of years the scene of continual pillage and massacre, so that the villages cannot be inhabited, the villagers nevertheless return whenever the power of peaceable possession revives. A generation may pass away, but the succeeding generations will return. The sons will take the place of their fathers, the same site for the village, the same position for the houses, the same lands will be reoccupied by the descendants of those who were driven out when the village was depopulated; and it is not a trifling matter that will drive them out, for they will often maintain their post through times of disturbance and convulsion, and acquire strength sufficient to resist pillage and oppression with success.

The village, as Metcalfe says, was a self-sufficing economic and social unit. It had an aristocracy of proprietors and their descendants, with a lesser group of cultivating tenants on various conditions. Below them again came the mere wage-labourers, probably of outcaste status, who lived apart from the main village and performed various menial duties, practised certain despised crafts like leatherwork, and did field work for the landholders. Linked with these groups were a circle of craftsmen and professionals. There was the village priest (Pundit or Maulvi), the record-keeper, the *bania* or shopkeeper and moneylender, the carpenter, the blacksmith, and so on. Women spun cotton and wove coarse cloth (*khadi*) and the men would do the same in off seasons. The village had its hall or meeting-place where the elders debated village affairs, arranging the revenue payments, carrying on relations with neighbouring villages, organizing the entertainment of visitors or strolling players, deciding the crops to be grown, settling disputes, and dealing with crimes according to customary laws. Communal watchmen guarded the cattle and watched the crops at harvest time. The typical village was practically self-sufficing and all it asked was to be left alone to extend its cultivation. But this was just what it was never allowed to do. Villages meant cultivation and cultivation meant revenue. The control of the land revenue was a prime objective of all Indian governments and, in consequence, their measures in dealing with them were the touchstone of Indian prosperity. No village, no revenue, has been the rule of Indian history.

The first requirement of the village was peace, and the next an equitable revenue assessment. After that all they asked was to be left alone. The British, confronted with the Moghul system as modified by time, wars, and successive 'splinter' states, had to decide how much to collect from the villages, and who should collect it. After realizing their first mistake, caused by their own ignorance, they drew heavily on Moghul experience. Eventually their own knowledge developed to the point where the comprehensive settlements initiated by Bentinck and carried through by Bird and others were possible. The question of collection was settled in various ways according to local conditions. In Bengal, the unwary Cornwallis and Shore mistook the existing hereditary tax-collectors for landowners and treated them as such, with the result that they created a new class of wealthy landholders at the expense of peasant proprietary rights, and many millions of lost revenue. This was the famous Permanent Settlement, one of whose few compensations has been the endowment of such patrons of culture as the Tagores and the Laws. Warned by this example the next settlement in Madras was made direct with each peasant. In the north settlements were largely made with whole villages at a time.

There remained the amount to be taken. The first mistake was over-assessment through a failure to take into account the amount of land under cultivation. The next was over-collection, a rigid insistence on realizing the demand in full, through a failure to understand the Indian habit of always asking for more than one expected to receive. The third mistake was seizure of lands on failure to pay. These things at first made British rule more unpopular than that of the rapacious Marathas, for though more just it was unsympathetic and though more regular it was rigid. But by the middle of the century these mistakes had been remedied through increasing knowledge, sympathy, and skill. Careful measurement and elaborate record-keeping kept disputes to a minimum, long-term assessments gave a sense of security, rebates for bad harvests and natural calamities gave the necessary elasticity. The first triumph of the revenue system was the calm of the countryside during the Mutiny; since that time it has secured a generally contented and prosperous peasantry and made possible a huge increase of population. The agrarian discontent which has occurred in some areas of recent years has been due to a change-over from subsistence to commercial farming, with the resultant dependence upon the fluctuations of world prices.

But one thing the British rule could not do—revive the age-old village community. Though this was the earnest desire of every British ad-ministrator, the goal proved elusive in proportion to the earnestness of the search. The more measures were taken, the more community life languished; perhaps the reason was the measures themselves. The village was a self-acting, self-contained organism, whose balance was upset by much outside influence. The intrusion of police, the establishment of courts, the appearance of paid officials all undermined the position of the village elders in the eyes of their fellows, and made them little more than ornaments for solemn occasions. Regrettable as the process was, it was caused rather by the inevitable centralizing tendencies of modern government than by any deliberate policy. Administrative measures only inadvertently hastened a process which was in fact largely inevitable.

With an ordered country, a code of laws, and a stable land revenue system, the Company had next to consider defence. The Company's army had been built up partly of British and partly of Indian troops, and Royal regiments were stationed in India as well. In course of time the Europeans disappeared from the Company's army, which became an Indian force of all arms officered by Englishmen. The proportion of

British troops to Indian declined until at the time of the Mutiny it stood at 1 to 8. Caste restrictions were carefully observed and a brotherly spirit prevailed between officers and men, but periodic mutinies showed how easy was the transition from military loyalty to religious fanaticism. The great Mutiny of 1857, arising from a particular grievance at a time of general unrest, set the seal on all the fears of the early empire-builders, and its suppression saw the recasting of the army in the form which persisted till recently. The artillery arm was abolished, Hindu, Muslim, and British troops were brigaded together, and the proportion of British to Indian troops was fixed at 1 to 2. The Indian army proper was reduced and its numbers fixed at 150,000. At the same time recruitment was limited to the 'martial races' (communities with a military tradition), with a bias towards Punjabis and the Frontiersmen. Gurkhas from Nepal were also freely employed under treaty. These measures were successful. An intense *esprit de corps* was developed among the men, who were kept occupied by constant frontier skirmishes. Not until after the reforms of 1921 were the first cautious steps taken to Indianize the office cadre. Until after 1940, when the great war expansion to over two millions inevitably gave the armed forces a national colour, the army was a closely organized professional body, well tempered to its purpose of guarding the frontier and guaranteeing internal order. It was the ultimate guarantee of the British control of India.

A word must now be said of the Princes. The Princes ruled rather more than two-fifths of the area and rather less than a quarter of the inhabitants of India. Their origin was very diverse and their frontiers confused and illogical. In order to facilitate the settlement of the country in 1818, the British recognized as Princes all those in *de facto* possession of the soil who were prepared to acknowledge their supremacy. There was a political moratorium; State boundaries were frozen as they existed at the moment, and remained substantially the same until 1947. This accounts for the extraordinary confusion of State frontiers in some parts of India, and for the great varieties in size and status of the various States. Thus Hyderabad, the largest of all, was really a fragment of the Moghul empire ruled by the descendants of a masterful Moghul governor; the States of Rajputana were clan chiefships whose history went back more than a thousand years; the Maratha States of Indore, Gwalior, and Baroda were remnants of the eighteenth-century Maratha military principalities; while Bhopal and other Central Indian states represented the enterprise of military adventurers in the time of troubles.

The British supremacy was maintained by the subsidiary forces in the large States already mentioned and by a system of Residents. Military support of the Prince meant not only freedom from foreign invasion, but freedom from internal checks. Lack of opportunity led to lack of enterprise and inertia and thus to misgovernment. This had been the chronic dilemma of British relations with the States. The Princes tended both to support and to discredit the paramount power. One solution was their absorption into British India as opportunity offered, but this, after a trial by Dalhousie, was dropped after the Mutiny. Another policy was then tried, that of modernizing the Princes in the hope that they in turn would modernize their States. This policy had some striking successes, as in the cases of Baroda and Mysore, and also some dismal failures. In general, it may be said that the States, with certain exceptions, were well behind the rest of India in all-round development. By maintaining the Princes after 1858, the British secured their steady support, but the failure to modernize and develop them, or to integrate them into the British Indian system as a whole, rendered that support passive instead of active. The policy of segregation and laissez-faire meant that the chance of modernizing India within a traditional framework was missed and that traditional institutions themselves became the objects of neglect and contempt. The princely order was an imposing but increasingly feeble prop of the British Dominion.

We have now surveyed the material bases of British power in India. There was peace for the country as a whole, ensured by an organized police; a legal system under which ordered court life could proceed with its panoply of courts and judges; a land system which ensured to the peasant a fair share of the fruits of his labour, and so encouraged him to further effort; a devoted army to guard the frontier and uphold the government; and a subordinate princely order to rule two-fifths of the country as imperial agents. All this would have served well enough in a stationary society; but other forces were at work and other ideas were knocking at the door, ideas which were to make all these arrangements appear to many as so many supports for reaction.

9
The Organization of Economic Life

THE TITLE OF THIS CHAPTER might be expected to be the Organization of Wealth rather than of economic life, on the analogy of those on
Power and Welfare. But the change has been made with deliberate purpose, because it serves to emphasize a certain difference of approach in
economic affairs, as distinct from those of welfare and political power.
In the sphere of politics the British deliberately constructed a positive
system of power, and in the realm of welfare they deliberately introduced
Western concepts and practices, even though they were careful not to
attack overtly Indian institutions. But in the field of economic life they
had no fixed plan before them and no fixed ideas to guide them. Rather,
perhaps, it might be said that the very idea they conceived was the
principle of having no fixed plan. Their system was to hinder hindrances,
their policy to leave each man free to promote his own welfare. So it came
about that modern Indian trade and industry, as distinct from the
traditional structure of rural economy, largely organized itself, with
important results both for the internal life of the country, and for the
attitude of India to the West. The British organized power, promoted
welfare, and made possible modern trade and industry.

The significance of this attitude was increased by the radical changes
which overtook economic techniques during the British period. The
British were the harbingers in India of the new industrial age, being
themselves its first beneficiaries and its apostles and agents overseas. Free
economic life therefore meant free play for the new portents of world
trade and mechanical production, a free entry on the traditional Indian
economic stage for the incalculable forces of world economy.

An understanding of British economic action and its consequences
involves some appreciation of the economic structure which the British

inherited from the Moghuls. Moghul economic organization was itself merely a variation of the traditional pattern of Indian economic life and it is therefore unnecessary to go further back. Indian economy, like that of most medieval states, was mainly a subsistence economy. But in the case of India the great size of the country and its well-defined geographical boundaries tended to accentuate a feature which the general conditions of the Middle Ages made inevitable. A subsistence economy was dictated to most states by the lack of means of large-scale production and the lack of cheap heavy transport. Trade of course there was, but it could only be in bulk where sea transport was available and cities stood close to the sea or on navigable rivers. So Rome was fed from Egypt, but even in this case the bulk of the traffic was small by modern standards. Trade was mainly in small-scale goods or luxury articles, for it was only those which could be carried cheaply enough for the general consumer or whose price could be paid by the rich.

The vast size of India made distance an even greater factor than in Europe. In addition there was a lack of navigable rivers or of easily-crossed inland seas to compensate for the lack of highways. Apart from the Ganges, which in peaceful times formed an artery of commerce from Bengal to Delhi and with the Brahmaputra provided Eastern Bengal with a network of waterways, and the Indus, which could have carried much commerce if only there had been commerce to carry, India is almost bereft of suitable waterways. The various empires maintained, when possible, highways primarily for military purposes, but there still remained the difficulties of expense and means of transport. It has been reckoned by Moreland that in the seventeenth century the cost of transport was 8 to 12 annas for 100 lb. per 100 miles exclusive of guards and custom duties, or at a rough approximation a shilling or twenty cents per hundred-weight per 100 miles. The cost of bulk articles doubled in 100 miles. When it is remembered that the ports of western India were often 500 miles or more from the main producing and consuming areas of the centre and north, and that there was in this region no other means of transport than road traffic, some idea of the difficulties of the medieval merchant can be gained. The limited means of land transport further constricted trade possibilities. The only wheeled traffic was the bullock cart, or in sandy regions the almost equally slow-moving camel cart. Apart from these there were only pack animals, the horse, the mule, and the camel while in hilly regions these were often replaced, as they still are in places today, by human transport. Special tribes engaged in the transport business are still to be found in out-of-the-way parts of the country at their old work. Only on the Ganges and the Jumna were conditions easier, where barges plied of up to 100 tons on the Jumna and 400 tons on the Ganges.

Finally, to these difficulties of transport and distance must be added those of political instability. Only for a few years between the seventh century A.D. and the Moghul period was India even nominally unified, and under the Moghuls it was barely unified by Aurangzeb before the disintegrating process was begun by the Marathas. Large areas in northern India during the later sixteenth and most of the seventeenth centuries did enjoy considerable periods of peace, but from the merchants' point of view there was a constant threat of danger and loss arising from political insecurity.

Indian economy under the Moghuls must be viewed against the general background of subsistence conditions and political instability. The basis of that economy was of course the peasant living in his self-contained and almost self-sufficing village community. Except in regions such as Gujarat and Bengal, where means of transport made commercial crops possible, he grew his own food while the village craftsmen wove his coarse cotton garments, built his mud or timber huts, carpentered his carts and woodwork, and worked his primitive minimum of ironwork. The village priest or *maulvi* presided at the temple or mosque, the record-keeper contributed an element of literacy, and the village headman with his council of elders formed a link with the government and outside world. The government appeared in the form of a revenue-collector, either directly through an official or through the agency of a noble to whom the village had been assigned in reward for service. In the south the agent was often a revenue-farmer, the most rapacious type of all. In either case the result was the same. The surplus wealth of the countryside was swept away to support the luxuries, policies, and wars of the various courts. The strength of a state could be reckoned in terms of land revenue just as today it can be reckoned in terms of industrial power.

In contrast to this basic fact of rural production and the appropriation of its surplus by governments, trade and industry, both local and foreign, played a subordinate part in the whole economy. This is not to say that they were unimportant, but that their limitations in bulk made them relatively less important to life as a whole than their modern counterparts. They attract attention because they were often picturesque, and we know a good deal about them because we possess travellers' reports and the records of foreign trading companies. But most of the trade and commerce, especially foreign trade, could have disappeared without vitally affecting the life of the Indian village. Indian industry, as already mentioned, can be divided into local and national. The former consisted of the local crafts and 'mysteries' which provided the villagers and small townsmen with their daily needs—coarse cotton cloth for clothing, earthenware pots for food and water, brass vessels, trinkets and jewellery for adornment and investment. The national industries centred round the princely courts and capitals ministering to the needs of the state and to the wants of the nobles. If not all articles in this trade were luxuries, few were indispensable, or made on a large scale, and these were usually centred in particular areas. Thus, sugar was refined in Bengal and Malabar where sea and river transport was available; indigo was manufactured in Gujarat partly for export; oil seeds were pressed (then as now) for illumination, tobacco was grown for all classes, and saltpetre produced both for cooling and gunpowder. The silk, calico, and muslin industries ministered to the upper official classes, and so did the luxury trades proper—gold and silver, ivory, metal, and woodwork. There was a shipbuilding industry which was confined to Surat on the west coast.

India conducted an active foreign trade within the limits of her transport and productive resources. Her great export was textiles, with which she supplied not only the European market, but also the Middle East and Indonesia as well. The textile trade was the key to India's export strength, and this explains the immense significance for India of the fact that the industrial revolution of the West began in the textile industry. Important subsidiary items were indigo (from Gujarat), spices (from Malabar), rice and sugar (from Bengal to the south), dyed yarn, and saltpetre. India had also a re-export trade, chiefly on the Malabar coast, in spices from the East Indies.

In return for these goods India imported horses from Arabia by sea through Goa to south India for military purposes, because good horses could not be bred there. There were raw materials for handicrafts, such as silk, ivory, coral, and amber; and there were certain basic metals such as tin from Malaya and zinc from Japan. There were luxuries and novelties such as precious stones (used on the Taj Mahal), spices, African slaves, Persian wines and carpets, Chinese goods, and European wines and novelties. But by far the most important items were the precious metals, particularly silver. Silver predominated for coinage and hoarding, and both gold and silver were used for display of all kinds. The golden plates of the Golden Temple of the Sikhs at Amritsar are a modern reminder of the habit, and the adornment of palaces and temples a witness to its long standing. 'Europe bleedeth to enrich Asia', feelingly wrote Sir Thomas Roe, English Ambassador to the Moghul court in 1616. 'India is rich in silver,' said his predecessor Hawkins, 'for all nations bring coin and carry away commodities for the same; and this coin is buried in India and goeth not out.' The bulk of this trade came and went by sea. The land traffic was reckoned in the early seventeenth century at 3,000 camel loads or 500 tons a year, and the sea traffic at a total of about 30,000 tons a year, which may be compared with an average of six and three quarter million tons of exports in the years 1911–1914.

Most of India's wealth—from agriculture, from industry, and from foreign trade—found its way to the Moghul government. After the heavy expenses of the Emperors had been met, with their propensities for display and building (to which the world owes the Taj and other great Moghul buildings), the balance went to maintain the régime, through its nobles and officials. The non-hereditary character of the Moghul official nobility and the confiscation of their estates at death led to lavish expenditure on their part on display, mosques, temples and tombs, and non-productive expenditure of all sorts. This mode of spending and the heavy import of the precious metals give the clue to the explanation of the legend of India's wealth in Moghul times. India *seemed* wealthy to the casual traveller who only visited the great cities, because of the lavish display to be found there and the well-known flow of silver into the country. But discerning travellers saw through the illusion even then; the acute Frenchman Bernier wrote to Colbert—'the inhabitants have less the appearance of moneyed people than those of many other parts of the globe'. In fact, India was then, as now, a poor country, though not perhaps relatively so poor in relation to the West as now. Great wealth was confined to a microscopic minority, and for the rest the great potential resources of the country remained undeveloped, owing partly to transport difficulties and still more to a social and political system which prevented any lasting accumulation of wealth and its use for productive purposes. Lack of transport was responsible also for the frequent famines which seared Indian life and devastated whole provinces, because surpluses from other parts of the country could not be moved in sufficient quantity or in time.

During the eighteenth century Indian economy was practically unregulated. The Moghul government lost its power and the East India Company had not taken its place. During the first half of the century foreign trade went on much as usual. The Company exported its cotton cloth, its saltpetre, and its indigo in increasing quantities, and added raw cotton to supply the nascent cotton industry in England. Indian calicoes and chintzes were frowned on in England, it is true, as rivals to the new home industry, but a flourishing re-export trade to Europe prevented this from being felt in India. In the second half of the century, however, two developments occurred which had the gravest effect on Indian economy. The re-export trade dried up owing to the series of European wars culminating in the Napoleonic struggle; and the Industrial Revolution transformed the output of the British cotton industry from a trickle to a flood. By 1760 England was exporting cotton goods to the colonies; by 1800 she was flooding the Indian market with *machine-made* goods.

It is at this point that the Company took control of India. The key to its economic policy is to be found, as in the case of its organization of power and welfare, in the ideas and forces to which it was subject at this time. There was first the official, sent to restore order in large tracts of devastated country. He was stimulated by the prospect of large-scale reconstruction, awed by the magnitude of the task, and impressed by the numerous signs, amidst the ruins of past administrations, of ordered design and ingenious adaptation of means to ends. The India of Malcolm and Munro, of Briggs and the Lawrences was a peasants' and princes' India; the desire of these men was to restore and improve the land system. Secondly, there were the economic theories which were influencing the controllers of policy both in Britain and India, and which were just beginning to pass from the stage of theory to that of practice in the sphere of actual administration. These were, of course, the free-trade and laissez-faire ideas derived from Adam Smith and propagated by the Utilitarians. James Mill was in the India House, to be followed by his son John Stuart, and if the Directors could see no sense in the promotion of free trade with India to the injury of their own monopoly, they could see every reason why the working of the monopoly itself should not be hindered by any artificial barriers. Thirdly, there were the groups of energetic traders and rising manufacturers who saw in India a market for their goods or a field for the investment of their new capital. It was the interaction of these three influences which determined British economic policy in India after the first disastrous period of drift, blunder, and experiment which covered the second half of the eighteenth century. It was a plan for the regulation of economic life in India rather than a positive plan for the development of Indian resources. It was an enabling rather than a mandatory plan; the Government's part was that of referee controlling a ring rather than that of an architect designing a temple of wealth.

Each of these groups, the official, the Utilitarian, and the trader and manufacturer played its part in the resulting organization of economic life and it is the clash of their various interests and viewpoints which explains most of the frictions and tensions of nineteenth-century economic policy in India. First came the local administrators. Their primary duty was the resettlement of the land and the reorganization of the land revenue system. Their work may be said to have begun in its regular form with the Permanent Settlement of Bengal in 1793, and it extended throughout India in a series of great measures over the first half of the nineteenth century. It is perhaps the greatest and most sustained effort of the British administrative genius overseas. Into details it is impossible to enter; it is possible to indicate only the broad lines of the process. Starting with the handicaps of insufficient knowledge and fallacious analogies with English conditions, the work was informed and redeemed by a steady determination to understand local needs and conditions, to retain the old where possible and to modify only in the light of equity. The purpose, beginning with the simple desire to settle the country and increase the revenue, ripened into the large design of giving the peasant security of tenure, encouraging the extension of cultivation, and easing the burden on agriculture so that the peasant could share in the profits of increasing prosperity. Generally speaking, this purpose has been achieved and is attested by a number of agreed facts. From 1903 to 1925, while agricultural prices rose 117 per cent., the land tax increased 20 per cent., the remaining increment going to the peasant, and this was admitted by a Committee of the Indian Congress in 1931. The Government's share of agricultural production sank from one-third or one-half in the eighteenth century to one-sixth or one-eighth in the twentieth century. The area of cultivation has increased so much that instead of landlords having to tempt tenants to their lands, as English lords had to do after the Black Death, peasants notoriously have to beg land from landlords or government. Instead of the desolation of waste or sparsely populated lands which confronted the early administrators, the signs of over-population began to appear from 1881 onwards. It is significant of the whole process that in all the criticism of recent years there has been no serious demand for land reforms except in the areas affected by the Permanent Settlement of Bengal, the first and admittedly the least satisfactory measure of the whole series.

During the nineteenth century, district officials constantly complained of the disturbance of local economy caused by the measures of the Supreme Government acting under orders from England. This brings us to the second formative influence on modern Indian life, current English economic ideas. These ideas were the Utilitarian ideas of free trade, free enterprise, and the removal of commercial barriers and restrictions. As they gathered strength in England and culminated in the free-trade régime from 1846 onwards, they inevitably influenced to an increasing degree the Indian administration. Not only were they enforced from above on a reluctant officialdom; they also seeped in among the officials themselves most open to new thought. Metcalfe and Elphinstone, Sleeman and Holt Mackenzie, all professed Utilitarian principles. Only the district officials, admiring traditional ways and thinking in terms of the old static economy, remained largely unaffected, and to them the attitude of Government seemed to be the fruit of an unholy alliance of English manufacturers and doctrinaire officials. These ideas ushered in for India a free-trade era. Internally much good resulted from the removal of trade barriers of all kinds. A landmark was the abolition of Inland Transit duties in 1835; in northern India great cactus hedges planted as customs barriers, and numerous old customs posts, still witness to former restraints. But externally the result was not so satisfactory. The free entry of Lancashire goods meant the end of the former flourishing textile industry of India. From 1850 onwards textile handicrafts were confined to the production of coarse cloth in the villages and handwoven luxury lines for the rich. The weaver mostly went back to the land, with incalculable loss to both art and production. India sank to the level of a colonial economy producing raw materials for others to manufacture and sell back to the country itself.

The third influence opened the way for the industrial development of India. The commercial interests of England forced their entry into India with the ending of the Company's trade monopoly in India by the Charter Act of 1813. Henceforward all were free to trade with India and in India. But freedom to trade does not necessarily involve ability to make profits. The new trader had no sooner arrived in India than he discovered that failure to develop the country was by no means entirely due to the Company's monopoly; nature's stranglehold was quite as effective as that of the perversity of man. The first few years of free entry, therefore, saw no sudden and rapid economic development. Instead there arose a cry for government interference. The interference demanded was not with the activities of the private trader, but with the obstacles to his trade. The government was to remove the impediments to free enterprise and so give the trader a fair field. This cry of the new entrepreneur, and the pressure he was able to exert on the government in

England, determined the nature of Indian commercial and industrial development during the nineteenth century.

The Government of India's part in the process may be described as that of 'enabling' action. It cleared the obstacles and 'enabled' the trader and industrialist to build up their own enterprises. This enabling action fell under four main heads—the land, commerce, communications, and finance. The object of the series of land settlements was not only to stabilize the countryside, but to make possible the extension of cultivation and to secure a steadily increasing revenue yield. The object of the commercial enabling action was to secure a free flow of trade, and this was obtained by removing trade barriers both internally and externally. These measures encouraged the growth of internal and external trade, but they could not in themselves create a flow of trade until further natural obstacles were overcome. This was why the years up to 1858 were mainly years of preparation rather than of large-scale economic achievement.

The great natural obstacle was still, as it had been in Moghul times, lack of transport, and the most important enabling action of the Government was the development of the modern Indian transport system. A road system was energetically undertaken from 1818 onwards, sometimes against the opposition of officials wedded to the old conditions. 'Metcalfe', wrote Lord William Bentinck sadly of his friend, 'has no idea of a good road.' Incidentally this remark illustrates the confusion of ideas often existing amongst the best of the Company's officials, for Metcalfe imagined himself to be a Liberal. Beginning with the Grand Trunk Road to the North-West Frontier, road building went on steadily until by 1927 there were 59,000 miles of first-class roads. Canals were also considered for this purpose, but by the time a network of irrigation canals (which could also be used for transport) had been constructed, they had been superseded as traffic arteries by railways. It was railways which effected the real transformation of the Indian transport system, and so made the development of the modern Indian economy possible. Their general plan was laid down by Dalhousie in his celebrated Minute of 1853. The system was state planned, state financially guaranteed, and in part state constructed; today, with a few insignificant exceptions, the whole of India's forty thousand miles of track are state owned and operated.

By means of railways, it was possible to link areas formerly divided by jungles, hilly tracts, and deserts. It was also possible to move heavy goods in quantities from one end of the country to the other. The results proved of incalculable value. The famine problem, most obstinate of

Indian economic ills, was solved so long as India remained self-supporting in the matter of food or could freely import from outside. The famine of 1876–78 was the last 'famine of plenty', and that of 1943 in Bengal the first famine of external scarcity. Trade was revolutionized by the opening up of the interior, which made possible special production for a market. Thus cotton and wheat, coal, iron, and other minerals could all be developed as never before. Above all, industries could grow both because coal could be supplied for power, and because the goods, once produced, could be moved to the markets. The raw materials of the Indian interior could at last be exploited, and India for both imports and exports came within the range of world economy. The whole process, and particularly the linking of India to the general world economy, was stimulated by the opening of the Suez Canal in 1869.

The last enabling measure of Government was the provision of financial facilities. The three Presidency Banks which were united in the Imperial Bank of India in 1921, reinforced by branches of the great British exchange banks, formed the steel frame of Indian commercial life. This system has since been completed by the Reserve Bank of India, now, like the Bank of England, a state institution.

The result of this enabling action was to make possible the indus-trialization of India. Because of the Government measures, industrializa-tion was made possible, and because of Government's failure to take the initiative, under the influence of laissez-faire ideas and pressure from interests in England, the process was delayed. Because Indian economy was linked to the British the initiative came at first from the British themselves, and because enterprise was free, Indians joined in as soon as they could overcome the handicaps imposed by low tariffs and the free competition of goods from the established industries of Britain. On the commercial side British trade developed that characteristic Indian organization, the managing agency, operating on the joint-stock principle. A managing agency is a commercial maid-of-all-work. It will undertake any work in any place for any one. The system has been used to sell goods of all kinds, to manage factories and plantations, and also to develop Indian industry by providing the management for Indian capitalists. In the industrial sphere, there have been developments of three kinds. The first are the plantation industries, such as tea, coffee, rubber, and tobacco, which grow and process their products on the spot. The second are the large crop industries, such as cotton and jute, which buy their raw materials from the cultivator and manufacture them in mills at industrial centres. The cotton industry has its main centres at Bombay and Sholapur in western India, Ahmedabad in Gujarat, and Kanpur in Uttar Pradesh and is mainly Indian-owned. The jute industry has its centre in Calcutta and is still largely British-managed. The third are the heavy industries, particularly coal, iron, and steel in Bengal and Bihar. Coal undertakings are still largely British-managed, but iron and steel are controlled by the great Indian corporation of Tatas, which produces more than a million tons of steel a year.

The period of free development may be said to have lasted until the first World War. Thereafter it was replaced by a régime of planned development under Government auspices. Its outward and visible sign was the recognition of the principle of Fiscal Autonomy in 1921 and its instrument the Tariff Board set up in 1923. By its means established Indian industries such as cotton were protected against 'unfair' competition and industries such as steel and sugar were fostered; it only needed the further stimulus of the second World War to set moving in full force the flowing tide of industrialization. But Britain could not, at one stroke, undo the economic and still more the psychological effects of a century's laissez-faire. The same liberty which had proved the secret of British industrial prosperity had converted India into a colonial economy, and it was only in response to the demands of the colonists themselves that industry in India developed. What has been condemned as deliberate British policy was in fact the normal working of current economic ideas and inevitable British economic pressures. But its effect on the Indian mind was the same as if the motive had been calculated egotism. It fostered a sense of dependence and of frustration and provided the key argument for a belief in the British exploitation of India. What was a plan to have no plan appeared in Indian eyes to be a regular design to retard the country's progress. Far more than the political actions of the British or their social plans, their economic planlessness bred the germs of ill-will between Britain and India. And the irony of the situation was that during the nineteenth century British economic policy in India was the one thing about which British administrators and statesmen alike were quite certain that they were right.

10
The Organization of Welfare

In ORGANIZING POWER the British were but following the precepts and to a large extent the practice of previous empire builders; for the organization of welfare there was little or no precedent. Previous empires had been content with the patronage of their own religion and culture; as for the people, their welfare was only a function of their capacity as revenue payers. The East India Company, if left to itself, would have been more neutrally minded about welfare, for it had no wish to promote even its own culture or religion. On the contrary, it had a lively sense of the danger of any interference with religious or social customs. Its ideal was essentially static—let everything proceed as before, and let the Company make its profits in peace. But the Company was not left to itself. It was subject to new currents of thought in Europe and England, which affected not only the British public and directors of policy, but also its servants themselves in India. It was the action taken as the fruit of these ideas which began the radical transformation of India whose culmination we have witnessed today. We have therefore to consider the ideas which formed the motives of British action, the measures which were taken to implement them, and the immediate effect of these measures upon Indian society.

At the beginning of the nineteenth century two streams of thought were influential in England, and they both made their influence felt in India. These were the Utilitarian and the Evangelical. The Utilitarians were the English expression of eighteenth-century rationalism; their watchwords were reason, utility, and the amiability of man, and they believed that no improvement was impossible if these principles were given free play. They were, in consequence, the sworn enemies of custom, vested interests, and privilege of every kind. Give free rein to human virtue and common-sense, they thought, and all would be well. When the Utilitarian looked to India he found a rich field for the exercise of his talents both of denunciation and construction. Everywhere, but more particularly in the Hindu system, he was confronted with privilege and age-old vested interests. Everywhere he found gross superstitition in the garb of religion. And since his moral standards were in fact the conventional Christian ethics of the time, he also found much for his conscience to deplore and his self-righteousness to condemn. In fact he found few things Indian to admire; his current comment was of a people sunk in superstition, apathy, and vice. At the same time his belief in reason and human good sense gave him a strong motive for interference.

Evangelicalism represented in England a revolt against rationalism and formalism in religion, and its practical outcome was a personal pietism with a severe code of conduct and a public humanitarianism which took its stand against the slave trade and a lead in social legislation. Through Wilberforce and Shaftesbury it was a force in public affairs. When the Evangelicals turned to India, they also found much of which to disapprove. Their repugnance to moral abuses and non-Christian ethics was even more lively than that of the Utilitarians, for they did not affect to be emancipated from Christian moral standards. It was reinforced by a horror of idolatry which was their own monopoly. But apart from deep 'disapprobation and animadversion' of heathen practices, there was another strong motive which drove them to India. This was their thirst for souls bound fast in Satan's chains. Thus the Evangelicals, like the Utilitarians, found little good in things Indian. Their current epithet for Hinduism was 'the abomination of heathenism' and for the Muslims 'infidel' and 'profligate'. Thus, both schools found good reasons to interfere in Indian affairs for the good of Indians themselves.

These two movements formed intellectual pressure-groups for reform and interference in India along Western lines. They were, each in their own ways, westernizing influences, tending to replace Indian customs, values, and ways of thought by European. They did not control the Government of India, but their influence ensured that when the Government moved at all, it would move along the lines which they had laid down. Together they constituted the Western challenge not merely to Hindu or Muslim power, but to Hindu and Muslim thought and culture also. Wellesley's victories meant no more to the Hindu or Muslim than Babur's or Taimur's, but the new ideologies were daggers pointed at the heart of both.

The direct influence of these schools in India can be gauged by a glance at their leading personalities. Jeremy Bentham himself was interested in India, and directly influenced men like Bentinck and Macaulay. His leading disciple, James Mill, occupied a key position in India House, and his standard *History of British India*, first published in 1817, made the Utilitarian thesis on India familiar to every student of affairs. His greater son, John Stuart, also spent his working life in the India House. Indian administrators, like Elphinstone, Holt Mackenzie, and even Metcalfe, were imbued with their ideas, which reached almost apostolic zeal in Macaulay's brother-in-law, the young Charles Trevelyan. The abolition of *sati* in 1828, the abolition of transit duties in 1835, and the education policy were direct results of their influence. On the Evangelical side the personalities were no less important. Charles Grant, who served the Company in Bengal and was later its Chairman, and his colleagues William Udney and Sir John Shore all belonged to this group. Grant was the friend of Wilberforce, who actively interested himself in Indian affairs and took a leading part in the Charter discussions in 1793 and 1813. The Evangelical chaplains, led by David Brown, reinforced by the Cambridge Senior Wrangler Henry Martyn and the Baptist Carey, influenced both the morals and the outlook of the Company's servants, and they were followed by the Presbyterian Alexander Duff and the Old Testament Christianity of the Punjab civilians. Henry Martyn, on hearing the sound of temple bells near his garden retreat in a Calcutta suburb, 'trembled at being in the neighbourhood of hell'; he regarded Roman priest and Muslim *maulvi* impartially as representatives of Antichrist. Together these men, in addition to influencing the Government, helped to launch Christian missions as a large-scale enterprise, with all its implications and incalculable effects.

Such were the ideas and influences which were permeating English society and modifying the declared Government policy of non-inter-ference and cultural laissez-faire. We have now to see how they bore fruit in action. The first step was an attack on obvious abuses, practices which, whatever their warrant in customs or sacred scriptures, offended against the universal moral law. The first of these was the suppression of child sacrifice on Saugor Island near Calcutta, a local if horrible custom which Hindu society generally condemned if it did nothing to suppress. Next came the much more widespread custom of infanticide, a practice encouraged by economic stringency and the dominance of the male in the Hindu social system, but not deeply rooted in Hindu ideology. The most spectacular of these measures was Bentinck's suppression of *sati* (or *suttee* as it used to be spelt) in 1829. This was the widespread and ancient custom (the Greek ambassador Megasthenes saw a *sati* at Pataliputra in the third century B.C.) of the burning of widows on the funeral pyres of their husbands. Unlike child sacrifice and infanticide, it had Hindu scriptural warrant. The sacrifice was supposed to be voluntary, but in practice was often enforced by fanatic or interested relations. Here Hindu opinion was divided, but Bengal accepted the abolition after a fruitless appeal to the Privy Council. It lingered on for many years in the north and west, and isolated cases still sometimes occur. Last in the list was the suppression of *thagi*, a combination of robbery with ritual murder to the glory of the goddess Kali. Though a definite Hindu cult it was detested by Hindus as much as by anyone else, since they suffered impartially with other communities. The evil spread with the breakdown of authority in Central India, but again it was Bentinck who grasped the nettle firmly and his agents Sleeman and Medows Taylor who rooted it out. Slavery, a recognized but not very widespread or oppressive institution in India, was finally abolished in 1843.

These measures appealed largely to Indian humanitarianism as well as to European, but we now pass to measures which, without directly attacking any cherished Hindu or Muslim institution or principle, subtly affected the whole structure of their thought. The first of these was education. Warren Hastings, encouraged by Sir William Jones and a band of Sanskritists, patronized Indian learning in the traditional manner. He founded Sanskrit and Arabic colleges, promoted the Royal Asiatic Society of Bengal, read Persian literature, and translated poems. In 1813 the Company was compelled by the Charter Act to spend £10,000 a year (at the then rate of exchange) on the promotion of learning in India. It was then that the new influences began to be felt. For some years the Company evaded its obligation, but when forced to recognize it, found itself faced with the problem of interpretation. What kind of learning and for what purpose? James Mill laid it down that by learning was meant 'useful knowledge', not the useless fables of Hindu mythology or the errors of the Koran. The crisis was resolved in 1835 by Bentinck with the help of Macaulay and his famous Minute. Henceforward the content of learning was to be European science and English literature and the medium of instruction to be English. The change was underlined by the simultaneous adoption of English instead of Persian as the language of Government business and in the higher courts of law.

The promoters of this great change knew quite well what they wanted to do. Bentinck, as early as 1829, wrote of 'the British language, the key to all improvements', and in 1834, before he met Macaulay, he wrote, 'general education is my panacea for the regeneration of India. The ground must be prepared and the jungle cleared away before the human mind can receive, with any prospect of *real* benefit, the seeds of improvement.' Macaulay was far more definite. He looked upon Hindu learning as a farrago of superstition and on Hindu knowledge as useless. The light of reason could never penetrate such heavy mists of prejudice and ignorance. Therefore a fresh start should be made with fresh minds using a new language before reason could work its perfect work. Supply reason and useful knowledge and Indians would then deal with their own superstititions for themselves. There would be, as Macaulay said in his Minute, 'a class of persons, Indian in blood and colour, but English in taste, in opinion, in morals and in intellect', and they would be the interpreters of Western civilization to the Indian masses. That such a class, when formed, might deliberately prefer the old to the new, did not occur to that penetrating but one-track mind.

If Macaulay's words meant anything, they meant a threat to the whole Hindu and Muslim intellectual structure. The agents were to be Indian it is true—'the body of interpreters'—but they were to serve just the same function in the mental war as Indian troops did in the physical. There was to be a conquest of the mind to match the conquest of the soil, and the mind (like the Indian states) was to be held by subsidiary forces—the new educated class. But besides the cultural and revolutionary conception, there was a political and utilitarian one, and it is the interaction of the two which has determined the course of Indian education. The Government needed a convenient linguistic medium for its growing administration and developing system of law. Hitherto, central business had been carried on in Persian and local affairs in local languages. English disinclination to learn languages made this system tend towards government by deputy with undue power to interpreters and secretaries. Utilitarian and Evangelical conviction of the superior qualities of Western and Christian civilization and Utilitarian conviction of the general 'usefulness of the English tongue' combined to secure the linguistic revolution of 1835.

The new policy was not, as might have been expected, strenuously opposed on the Indian side. On the contrary, there was support and even enthusiasm for it, and opposition came only from the professors of the old studies, whose position was rather like that of the advocates of compulsory Greek at Oxford and Cambridge. This support was of two kinds. There was the practical desire to master English because its knowledge gave good prospects of worldly success. And there was the intellectual desire to master English as the key to the new knowledge of the West. The great Bengali, Ram Mohan Roy, to whom we shall be referring again, was the protagonist of this view. The practical view was held by many otherwise orthodox people, and its force was seen in the numerous English schools which sprang up at that time. The theoretical view was the vision of a group of forward-looking intellectuals. Both united in the foundation of the Hindu College of Calcutta (1816), the first modern college of university standing.

The immediate result was a release of mental energy. Western science became a new gospel, and its devotees displayed religious enthusiasm. The first dissection by a Hindu student was a solemn act performed in the spirit of devotion, and a poet could boast of dreaming in English. In distant Delhi the new spirit infected the Muslim greybeards of the Moghul circle and set Maulvis Zakaullah and Nazir Ahmad translating Western works. But in general the practical demand for English as a means of livelihood tended to obscure the implications which knowledge of the language involved, and it was practical considerations which were increasingly in the mind of the Government. The increasing demand for English knowledge was met by a system whose lines were laid down in Sir Charles Wood's (Lord Halifax's grandfather) dispatch of 1854. A hierarchy of state-aided schools led to colleges and universities of the examining type organized on the London model, the first three of which were founded in the year of the Mutiny, 1857. At the same time the Government made the B.A. a necessary qualification for higher government employment. In consequence those who wanted government service, with all the prestige which it carries in the East, had to go to college, and those who went to college looked to government service because there was little else they could do. A certain drabness descended on the educational system; the grey clouds of utility blighted the prospect of intellectual renaissance. The new education was useful and very little else. Macaulay's 'interpreters' of the West to the Indian masses came to learn even their mathematical problems by heart. 'Baboo' English was no accident or Indian eccentricity, but the natural result of overlaying the spirit of the West with the paste of utility. Men perceived the Western culture as through a glass darkly, and originality was distorted to imitation. The arts were neglected as 'frills', and the graces despised as 'light'.

The last eighty years have seen a series of attempts to correct the balance, to humanize, to broaden, and to deepen. The first agents of this process were the educational missionaries. The first Christian Arts

College, apart from Danish Serampore, was the Scottish Churches College founded by Alexander Duff in 1835, and soon India was covered with a network of Christian institutions within the official framework. America took up the tale and contributed such great figures as Ewing of Lahore. Educational missions attracted numbers of able and devoted men and women, who infused a new spirit into the system while keeping within it. The residential system, the personal concern of teachers for the taught, the reorganization of community life based on Christian principles, all tended to provide a moral and spiritual background to the mental tread-mill of the government system. In the educational as in other spheres of life, the missionary influenced by promoting moral and spiritual progress along Western lines.

The Government itself was not inactive, and was increasingly in-fluenced by the ideas of Indians themselves. Various attempts, not con-spicuously successful, were made to extend primary education. In 1902 Lord Curzon sought to reform Calcutta University along the lines of the London reforms; he promoted residential institutions and post-graduate studies and tried to raise standards by stricter control of the colleges. In 1919 the Sadler Commission proposed a new series of teach-ing and residential universities. Two years later education was handed over to Indian control as a 'transferred subject' under the Montford reforms. Under this impulse the number of universities rose from five to thirteen, distinctions were increasingly made between pass and honours courses, research was undertaken, and technical courses of all kinds were developed. Research institutions like the Indian Institute of Science at Bangalore and the Agricultural Research Institute at Pusa (now at New Delhi) were set up. Without losing its utilitarian complexion in its lower ranks, Indian higher education has increasingly approximated to the standards of the West. Her universities became more than examining bodies and many of her colleges better than cram shops. Her scholars are striking out for themselves, and many of her professors are of world repute.

But we must now return to other embodiments of the concept of welfare. In the sphere of law, the English concept of equality found expression, and this was also a revolutionary change. Within Hinduism there had always been one law for the caste man and another for the outcaste, and often, like clerical claims in the Middle Ages, one law for Brahmins and another for non-Brahmins. Muslim law also distinguished between Muslims and infidels, both in matters of procedure and status. Under the new régime all were equal and though the equality was at first often nominal it was something which has progressively become more real. In the interests of this principle the Hindu law of inheritance in Bengal was modified in 1832 by a regulation allowing those who changed their religion to retain their property, and this was enforced in 1850 for the whole of India. In 1856 a Widow Remarriage Act allowed Hindu widows to retain their rights on remarriage, another breach of orthodox custom. But more important than all enactments, perhaps, was the enforcement of the rule of law impartially by the Courts, and the upholding of the individual's rights as an individual.

In the sphere of rights and law, British reforms were restrained by the maxim of non-interference. Their work was in the main negative rather than positive, a cautious suppression of abuses or removal of disabilities rather than the large-scale introduction of new principles. But in the material sphere there was no such inhibition. The Anglo-Saxon mind and conscience, both in its Utilitarian and religious forms, turned with relief from the intricacies of Hindu and Muslim personal law to the practical philanthropy of material welfare. The most obvious material evil in India was the recurrent famines. These have devastated parts of India periodically through recorded history. The lack of large-scale inland transport, owing to the absence of inland waterways (except in Bengal), made each region dependent upon itself for food. Over most of India it was impossible to bring supplies at all or to bring them in time to relieve distress. If the crops failed, people must suffer and die where they stood. The first symptom of famine was the selling of peasants into slavery, and every big famine was accompanied by large-scale depopulation. Between 1605 and 1660 an incomplete list gives twelve famines in different parts of the country. One devastated the Punjab as far as Delhi; the Gujarat famine of 1630–31 so reduced the indigo growers and cotton weavers that it took nearly ten years for the province to recover. The famine of 1782 in the Delhi region swept away quite half the population, and twenty years later many villages were still deserted on the British occupation. The Emperor Akbar attempted some relief in the great famine of 1595–98 but there was little he could do, and the usual reaction was apathy and resignation to the will of God. In early British times the same feeling of helplessness prevailed, so that even the benevolent Sleeman argued against forcible procurement of grain on the ground that it would only drive the *banias* to bury whatever stocks they had and so make things worse.

The disastrous Orissa famine of 1866, which the local officials failed to forecast, followed by others in the seventies, brought matters to a head. The result was the famine code following the great Famine Commission of 1880. The essence of the system was the timely forecast of probable shortage and the bringing in of supplies from other parts of India or overseas. Once this had been done, relief became a matter of organization and administration. Special officers controlled the distribution of supplies. Private trade was left unfettered as far as possible. To avoid pauperization, relief works were organized on which the cropless peasants could occupy themselves and earn a livelihood. Recovery was assisted by remission of land revenue so that the peasant would not experience an aftermath of hopeless debt. The cost was covered by a central famine fund on which distressed areas could draw when necessary. By these means famine in the old sense was banished from the turn of the century until the Bengal famine of 1943. Crop failure occurred as before, but now a famine meant a famine 'of work rather than of food'. The Bengal famine demands a word to itself. It was essentially the result of war conditions: the initial shortage was caused by the cutting off of Burmese rice owing to the Japanese occupation; alternative supplies were unobtainable owing to war conditions; and the situation was aggravated both by floods and consequent transport difficulties and by an administrative breakdown of the popularly-elected provincial government.

It will be noticed that the essence of famine relief was the transfer of supplies from surplus to deficit areas. This involved transport. The conquest of famine has therefore to be closely linked with the development of railways. The first example of their efficiency was the famine of 1860 in the present Uttar Pradesh. The new railways brought the necessary food and converted this visitation into the first famine of 'work rather than of food'. Henceforward the development of railways was pursued with an eye to famine prevention, though economic development was of course their main motive. The significance of railway development in general has already been discussed.

The second important factor in famine prevention is the supply of water in areas of uncertain rainfall by means of irrigation. In ancient India kings paid much attention to this science, and Central and Southern India are dotted with great tanks or reservoirs designed to retain monsoon water for use in times of scarcity. The Muslim kings of the north, including Firoz Shah and Shah Jehan, constructed some canals, including one to Delhi. But nearly all these works had long been disused on account of political troubles and the lack of resources to maintain them. The British began by restoring some of the derelict works. In 1820 water ran through the Moghul canal to Delhi once more, and the population turned out in gala dress to welcome it. There followed original works. The Grand Anicut, undertaken in 1835 across the bed of the Cauvery river in South India, has a length of two miles; the Ganges canal, the first great work in the north, was described by Dalhousie in 1856 as being 'unequalled in its class and character among the efforts of civilized nations'.

Development has gone on ever since. The Godavari system has a total length of 2,500 miles, the Upper and Lower Ganges canals of 8,000 miles. In the Punjab alone the area irrigated is twice that of the whole Egyptian system. The great Sukkur Barrage in Sind, first opened in 1932, was designed to irrigate three million acres of waste land. By 1947 in British India canals irrigated $32\frac{1}{2}$ million acres, or one-eighth of the total cultivated area. The canals have done much more than safeguard areas of doubtful rainfall from famine, they have caused millions of acres of rainless waste land to blossom like the rose. Canal colonies, with their robust, prosperous, and forward-looking inhabitants, are now a regular feature of Indian life.

Finally, mention must be made of the Indian health services. Hindus and Muslims both have their medical systems, the one derived from ancient Sanskrit texts, and the other, as its name *Yunani* implies, coming from the Greeks. Both include a wide knowledge of medical herbs and an extensive physical lore, but neither has any pretensions to surgery or, of course, to antiseptic medicine. In the towns are to be found skilful and learned Indian doctors, but there is little effort to maintain standards, and the country practitioner tends to be a little better than the medieval medical quack. He is, in fact, the Middle Ages in working order. Medical science was introduced along with other branches of western knowledge, and in the Calcutta Medical School young Hindus in anguish faced the dilemma between the claims of new knowledge and the demands of orthodox purity. Knowledge won, and today there is a thriving Hindu and Muslim Western medical profession, whose surgeons can vie with the West in skill. In 1938 there were ten medical colleges with 1,800 students, and twenty-eight medical schools; many in addition went direct to the West for training. There were upwards of 40,000 Western-trained doctors. Besides the medical profession itself, there was a steady development of health services on Western lines. The Government established a network of hospitals and increasingly interested itself in health services and disease prevention. Much has been done to bring smallpox, cholera, and plague under control, and a good deal, though not yet enough, to crush malaria. Public Health officers have been appointed, and sanitation schemes have transformed the great Indian cities from sinks of pestilence 'where two monsoons were the life of a man', into tidy and well-kept towns. If anti-flush societies still exist, and pious people will still let plague-infected rats out of their cages in deference to the sacred principle of life, modern measures have in general gained acceptance by their results.

It remains to consider the effect of these efforts on Indian society. It was neither so revolutionary as had been hoped, nor so negligible as had been feared. But it was both perceptible and significant. Briefly, these measures, along with those described in Chapter 8, may be said to have created new social conditions which made the emergence of new forces possible when Indians themselves had begun to decide their attitude to the European cultural invasion. The first effect was a change in the social balance, in the relations of the various classes. The old landowning or rent-collecting aristocracy and the old official classes tended to recede into the background. The new land settlements often impoverished them; there was no avenue to honour and fame in government service because, until 1835, no Indian could hold a post worth more than 500 Rupees a month under the Company. These men withdrew within themselves and, even when not financially embarrassed, spent their lives dreaming of past glories, composing mournful odes, and cultivating self-pity. Not for them the surgeon's knife, the scholar's grammar, or the administrator's desk. There was, in fact, no place for them as such in the new society and they lacked the intellectual vigour to study English for its own sake.

In their place arose the new middle class, the most significant creation of the British in India. Designed to be the interpreters of the West to the East, they became in fact the oracles of the East on the strength of their Western knowledge and, so, the potential supplanters of the British. The new middle class was the composite product of all the constructive policies of the British. The unification of the country made the system of government uniform, the new government demanded an English-knowing class for its administration, and a science-knowing one for its new services like the railways, road engineering, and irrigation. Later, the expansion of trade and industry created a further demand for clerks and technicians. The new educational system provided the facilities needed for this, and the prestige attached to government service in turn ensured a plentiful supply of students in the colleges. At the same time railways encouraged travel and communication all over India. Government posts and the opportunities awaiting the adepts of the new learning established Bengali colonies in all the chief cities, and these in turn were centres of the new ideas. The class as a whole was a subordinate class, ministering to the fiat of high European officials; but it contained certain independent elements, from which leadership was eventually to germinate. These were the lawyers, the doctors, the teachers, and the professors. Slowly as Indianization proceeded, the higher ranks of the official hierarchy were penetrated by members of this class, but it was, and still is, from the independent professions that modern Indian leaders have developed: Gandhi, Nehru, Patel, and Jinnah were all lawyers.

This fertile bourgeois soil was steadily watered from a common cloud of ideas. Throughout India similar colleges studied the same books. Shakespeare, Milton, and the Bible in literature; Burke, Mill, and Macaulay in politics; the Magna Carta, the Long Parliament, and freedom broadening down through history—in fact the whole liberal gospel—were the mental food for the new generation of aspiring Indians. Along with literary masterpieces came democratic ideas and philanthropic enthusiasm, Utilitarian pleas for rational reform, and Christian zeal for moral righteousness. New standards and new values, new conceptions of society and ideas of individual worth, all jostled in the student's mind in the course of learning English. On many it had no effect; on many more it seemed to produce parallel sets of Eastern and Western ideas held in separate compartments of the mind, and typified by the custom of wearing European clothes to office and Indian clothes in one's home. But the ferment was going on, though only the higher minds were fully conscious of it. For all the external calm of the nineteenth century, India was locked in deadly mental fight. What was to be her attitude in the Western cultural invasion? Should it be accepted, or rejected, or absorbed and synthesized?

11
The Indian Response

IT IS A COMMON AND SERIOUS MISTAKE to suppose that the Indian response to the impact of the West was an automatic reaction to external stimuli. Place books before Indians and they will learn to read; lay down a railway track and they will learn to drive; give them scalpels and they will learn to operate; establish parliamentary institutions and they will learn to govern themselves: these are the unconscious assumptions of much intelligent but casual approach to the country. Indian civilization is allowed to have borne the fruits of intelligence and adaptability, so that Indians can be expected to do and like the things we do and like ourselves; it is not allowed to have developed a world view and a scale of values of its own which have a separate existence of their own and are entitled to respect and study. But that is precisely what India has. An Indian is applauded if he becomes an authority on biochemistry or writes a book on currency problems, but he is thought rather old-fashioned and 'oriental' if he studies his own classical literature, and distinctly back-ward if he takes seriously the precepts of his own philosophy. Yet the intellectual and moral background of Indian civilization is as real and valid to the Indian as ours is to us, though many Indians, like many Europeans and Americans, may be but dimly aware of its precise nature. There was no *tabula rasa* of the Indian mind, no clean slate on which the moving finger of progress could write, and therefore there could be no joyous embrace of a new revelation such as an African of the primeval forest or a South Sea islander might experience. The coming of Western knowledge meant ferment and conflict, a mental war which was none the less dramatic for lacking the clang of violent outward action. The drama of the nineteenth century Indian was that of the chess player, absorbed and exhilarated by an exciting mental problem. How was India, with her ancient ways and deeply considered philosophies, to treat the new knowledge and modes of thought which flowed in through her foreign-controlled and embarrassingly duty-free mental ports? It is around the answer to this question that the story of modern India is built up, and it is on the solution of this problem that the present and future of India depend.

It is said that when the first Anglican bishop arrived in Calcutta, in 1814, the Brahmins there were in some apprehension. Might he not be the harbinger of the new rulers' religion and have come to subvert their long supremacy? Observers were sent to watch the intruder, but when they reported that the good bishop lived in state resembling that of a member of council and in manner of life indistinguishable from other officials they set their fears at rest, content that the intruder had no religion worth the name. But therein they erred, for the new ideas came by other than episcopal channels—through grammars and text-books, through schools and government offices and law courts, through a foreign literature and daily contact with foreign officials. The English are a secular people, but they carry their week-day religion wherever they go; every Englishman was an unconscious apostle of Anglo-Saxondom, as later in China every American was a prophet of Americanism.

India was first aware of the Western challenge in the eighteenth century as a political threat of power. That challenge was settled by the establishment of British supremacy in 1818, and India did not stir, because political power was far from the centre of Hindu life and thought. If A wants X and B cherishes Y, B will be unmoved when A acquires X so long as he retains Y intact. It was only then that the real challenge began—the intellectual challenge of Western knowledge and science based upon the unfettered working of reason, the moral challenge of Christian standards and ways of living, the psychological challenge of European self-confidence, exultant with its ever-increasing control of nature and its deepening penetration of the empire of the mind. Looked at from this angle the whole of modern Indian development falls into place as an ordered series of responses to a set of challenges as pervasive and subtle as Brahmin philosophy itself. The responses were empirical, and they were all designed to one end, the attainment of a *modus vivendi* with the new spirit without the loss of self-respect to the Indian mind and soul.

Since reaction must be a result of the original action, the first Indian response was military. Indian princes reflected upon the apparent magic of European arms and discipline, of European cohesion and ability to subordinate personal interests to a common purpose. Military efficiency, they concluded, was the talisman of Western success. Like the Turks a little later, they hoped to stave off the European menace by developing a comparable military technique themselves. European arms and discipline were copied, European adventurers were engaged to train and direct the troops. Indian armies ceased to be bands of military adventurers surrounded by hordes of camp-followers and clouds of plunderers. Disorderly feudal arrays like that of the Nizam in 1750 gave place to the disciplined battalions with which Mir Kasim attempted to prevent the European domination of Bengal in 1763, and these again to the efficient corps of the French general de Boigne in the service of the Maratha chief Sindia in the eighties. Only when these failed against Lake and Wellesley, though not essentially for military reasons, did the Marathas revert for a time to their old guerrilla tactics. The last and greatest of these military efforts was the Sikh army of Ranjit Singh in the Punjab. Its discipline was equal to that of the Indian Army and its artillery was more deadly; had other factors besides the purely military been equal, the Sikh wars of a little over a hundred years ago might well have had a different result. But other things were not equal. The Indian princes had left out of their calculations the cohesive spirit of the West, which made their armies the servants of civil directors and prevented soldiers and civilians alike from splitting up into rival factions of adventurers. An Indian soldier could not resist the temptations of personal power, for there was nothing in his system to hold him back. Above all, they lacked the economic power of the West, which enabled it to pay disciplined forces regularly and replace armies which had been destroyed. Disciplined troops without pay were more dangerous than the old levies; they had no estates or old jobs to fall back upon and so turned their arms on their employers. Arrears of pay and personal ambitions formed the graveyard of Indian military hopes.

The next response may be called the conservative or reactionary. Its cry was the prophet's 'Come ye out from among them', and the attitude was that of Bunyan's pilgrim hastening from the City of Destruction with his fingers to his ears. The West was admittedly stronger, said the conservatives, but its ideas were dangerous and its manners odious. Let not the true Indian, Hindu or Muslim, compromise with the evil thing. They should withdraw themselves, so far as they were able, from contact with the foreigner, and live their own lives in the traditional way. This reactionary spirit took many forms and is still to be found today—in full force in religious centres like Benares or Nadia, and in out-of-the way parts of the country—and to some extent in the mind of nearly every Indian. In the religious sphere it inspired the opposition to such measures as the suppression of *sati* and the glorification of customs which in other circumstances the apologists themselves might have led the way in modifying. Like slavery in the Southern States when threatened from the North, half-recognized abuses became 'peculiar institutions'. In the intellectual sphere it strengthened a blind reliance on textual authority, 'the traditions handed down once for all to the saints'. Unable to answer the new ideas because unwilling to consider them on their merits, the champions of the past resorted to a sterile doctrine of authority. Caste rule was immutable, the Muslim law unalterable. Politically, it coloured the outlook of the Indian Princes in the considerable territories they still controlled. One symptom was the nostalgic veneration for the now shadowy Moghul authority, another a longing to revive the ancient glories of Hinduism, and a third a preference for corrupt Indian rule to British order and security. It was among the Princes themselves that the idea worked itself out and demonstrated its bankruptcy. Like Red Indian chiefs, confined to reservations, cut off from the best, but in contact with the worst from the new world beyond, they retained all their old life except its vivifying purpose. They were protected not only from their enemies, but also from their subjects. They had their rights, but no duties or responsibilites; autocracy was no longer tempered by the fire of public danger or the water of public criticism. There was no outlet for their ambitions and no sanction for their good behaviour. The inevitable result was apathy verging towards vice, and stagnation verging towards anarchy. The States drifted further and further away from the main-stream of modern life, and steadily approached the status of museums more or less picturesque and more or less tidy. The first seventy years of the nineteenth century in the States proved that in a moving world the 'stand fast where you are' principle means in practice a steady retro-gression.

The supreme expression of the reactionary spirit was the Mutiny of 1857. In one tense and tragic moment all the country's love of its old way of life, regret for past glories, and distrust of and disgust at foreign innovations flared up in a violent explosion of emotional resentment. The actual occasion for the outbreak, the issue of cartridges greased with the fat of pigs and cows, was nicely calculated to irritate both communi-ties in singularly tender spots, but the blunder, great as it was, would have been retrieved if there had not been a pre-existing atmosphere of sus-picion and ill-will. This atmosphere was itself the expression of the conservative reaction against interference and foreign innovation. There was Dalhousie's eager annexation of Indian states under the pretext of the Doctrine of Lapse, which seemed directly to threaten all the remaining refuges of traditional Indian life. There was the large-scale resumption of rent-free tenures, which seemed to thousands downright confiscation. There were Western innovations like the telegraph and railways, which offended orthodox sentiment and by their convenience put a premium on the breaking of caste rules. There was the new education with its subversive ideas, and the preaching of increasing numbers of missionaries, by no means always conciliatory. The rising, when it came, revealed in its development the conservative nature of the forces behind it. The Muslims rallied round the aged Moghul Emperor at Delhi, the Hindus round the heir of the last Maratha Peishwa at Cawnpore. The heroic Rani of Jhansi wanted simply to recover her lost principality. And the abstainers from the Mutiny were as significant as its abettors. The Nizam wanted no restored Moghul authority, for he was himself an hereditary *de facto* rebel from the authority of Delhi. The Maratha Princes equally wanted no revived Peishwaship to exercise authority; policy therefore triumphed over sentiment and kept them loyal, or at least neutral. The Sikhs had so lively an objection to Moghul authority that they were actively loyal, though they had been decisively defeated by the British less than ten years before. The countryside in general remained quiet because Western innovations had so far affected them little and the British were at least no more oppressive than their predecessors. Above all, the rising middle class with their Western education were actively on the side of the British, because their prospects and position in society were bound up with the survival of the new order. So far from being the first war of independence or a national revolt in the modern sense, the Mutiny was the final convulsion of the old order goaded to desperation by the incessant pricks of modernity. In its passion and futility it was a *Fronde* rather than a *Risorgimento*.

The next response was that of acceptance. There were those among the intellectuals in touch with the British who were dazzled by the new ideas. The new light in their eyes was so bright that they thought the light within themselves was darkness. They took, so to speak, Macaulay at his word, and set out to westernize themselves in thought, mind, and spirit; they formed beef-eating clubs and gloried in the defiance of caste 'superstition'. Like Renaissance scholars with their Greek, they treasured the purity of their English accent. They had a double inspiration. One was the rationalist, coming from Hume, Bentham, and the Utilitarians. This had its English representative in Calcutta in David Hare the watchmaker, and its leader in the Anglo-Indian Derozio, whose short candle of life burned with a tragic brilliance reminiscent of the boy-poet Chatterton. The other was the religious inspiration of Christianity. The religion of the West, as expounded by the Baptist Carey and the Scotch Presbyterian Duff, seemed to them to fill the moral gap which the religious side of Hinduism had left vacant. So for a few years there was a stream of Brahmin and other high-caste converts, whose descendants are to be found today in leading positions in the Christian community.

The advocates of acceptance rather than the mutineers were the real revolutionaries of nineteenth-century India. Once that is said, it is easy to understand the fading away of their movement; for, whatever may have at times been done or said to the contrary, India is essentially a conservative country. They have generally been regarded as eccentrics, but they were perhaps only rather more than a century ahead of their time. The massive conservatism of India was the fundamental cause of their eclipse. It needed far more external pressure than had yet been applied to induce India to consider seriously such a drastic alternative. Surely, argued subconsciously the average intelligent Hindu, there must be some half-way house between wholesale acceptance or wholesale rejection of the West, some *modus vivendi* which will give us some of the worldly advantages of the new order without forfeiting the spiritual comfort of the old. We may have sunk low, murmured collective Hinduism, but not so low as to deny our caste, our *dharma*, our Mother India herself. Along this line India has been feeling her way ever since. The ethic of acceptance, based on the cults of reason and Christianity, has never died out, but it has been a creed for individuals, not for groups. In recent years it has had a marked though hardly noticed revival on a new foundation and from an unexpected quarter—the Communists. Marxist materialism is as uncompromising, as totalitarian in its claims and as un-Indian as rationalism or Christianity ever was, but so far its intellectual influence has been limited.

The conservative response was too comfortless and the radical response too drastic for Indian needs and tastes. India then looked within herself for the secret of renewal. This may be called the orthodox response, the attempt to find the secret of new life in the neglected portion of her own religious heritage. It was a 'back to the Fathers and the primitive church' movement, an attempt to cut away the accretions of the ages, the fustian of habit and custom, and so to reveal the Hindu spirit in its pristine beauty and vigour. The well of living water was there, but it was choked with briars and weeds; the light shone, but it was under a bushel of superstition.

The first of these efforts was the Brahmo Samaj, founded by the Bengali reformer Ram Mohan Roy in 1829. We shall have more to say of this encyclopaedic mind a little later, but here we are concerned with his work as a Hindu reformer. The 'Society of God' was a reform group within Hinduism. It appealed to the Hindu scriptures, but only to those scriptures which appealed to it. It accepted the Western concept of reason, but found that concept in the Hindu philosophical treatises known as the Upanishads. It urged the reform of Hinduism, but on grounds of Hindu not European rationalism. A master of eight languages, and a reasoner of sufficient force to convert a missionary to Unitarianism, Ram Mohan Roy could out-quote the pundits with Sanskrit texts and out-argue the moderns in the field of logic. The Samaj proved the real counter to the acceptance school and for a time was a real moral and intellectual force. But it was narrowly theological in its outlook and failed when it came to interpreting the whole modern experience in terms of Hindu thought. One half of the society then became semi-Christian and the other relapsed into philosophical quietism.

Next came the Arya Samaj, founded in 1875 in the Punjab by an ascetic of the traditional type, Swami Dayananda. As befitted its place of origin, Dayananda's message was a militant assertion of primitive Hinduism. His cry was 'Back to the *Vedas*', the earliest Hindu scriptures, in which he believed were to be found all knowledge, all holiness, and all truth. The Vedas were verbally inspired, like the Protestant Bible, and Dayananda would have been at home in the disputatious atmosphere of seventeenth-century Europe. Dayananda was not content with verbal inspiration. His message included denunciation of idolatry and caste, a drastic simplification of ritual, and a return to the primitive discipline of *brahmachari* and the four stages of life, of the 'piety, endurance, and devotion' of ancient India. His movement had a wider and deeper appeal than that of the Brahmo Samaj. It possessed the secret of all successful moral movements—a call to self-discipline and sacrifice—and it salved much wounded Hindu pride with its pictures of the past glories of Hinduism. Today it numbers about half a million adherents, mainly in the Punjab, and has had marked success in such matters as the raising of the marriageable age, the education of girls, the improvement of the status of widows, and the removal of minor taboos. It inspired a new self-respect which often developed into militancy like the *shuddhi* or reconversion movement. But it has not swept Hinduism or solved its pressing problem of accommodation with the West. The reason for this lay in its intellectual limitations. It was a cult of authority and it suffered the same embarrassment in the face of rationalism and the scientific spirit as ultramontane Catholicism or fundamentalist Protestantism. It could prove no satisfaction for Indian minds touched with Western scepticism.

Another attempt was the enthusiastic piety of the Krishna devotee Ramkrishna (1834–86). His disciple Vivekananda tried to find an intellectual foundation in the philosophic system of the Vedanta and a moral basis in the imitation of Christian good works with the Ramkrishna mission. This movement has failed on the intellectual side by falling into the attractive but enervating fancy of the oneness of all religions. If this made Hinduism the equal of other religions it also made other religions the equals of Hinduism. The removal of the talisman of uniqueness was not the way to kindle an aggressive spirit or strengthen self-respect. Its greatest success was Vivekananda's appearance at the World Congress of Religions at Chicago in 1893. The Maratha politician Tilak made another attempt by combining the exploitation of orthodox sentiment with Western political technique. Here the two sides of the programme were too obviously uncorrelated and the range of appeal was too narrow.

On the Muslim side there were comparable movements which failed to satisfy for much the same reasons. The Wahabi movement had the moral force of a return to primitive Islam but lacked any relation to Western thought. The more recent Ahmadiya movement of the Punjab was more forward and socially progressive, but alienated orthodox feeling by setting up another prophet besides Mohammad, and failed to meet the demands of rationalism because it appealed to authority based on a new revelation. The old lights shone again, but they could not obscure the glare of the West.

There remained the solution of synthesis which may be called the working faith of modern India. It is the work primarily of two creative minds, Ram Mohan Roy amongst the Hindus and Syed Ahmad Khan for the Muslims. Both had their roots in traditional culture, both responded eagerly to the new ideas without losing faith in the essence of their own tradition, and both believed that East and West could be combined, not merely mechanically and superficially in the world of action, but integrally and organically in the realm of thought. It is therefore worth while to examine these two men a little more closely, for in them is to be found the ideological secret of modern India.

Ram Mohan Roy was a Bengali born in 1772. In youth he wandered in the traditional way in search of enlightenment and broke with his family on the issue of Hindu abuses. He then took service with the East India Company, where he came into contact with British people and Western ideas. For the last eighteen years of his life (from 1815 to 1833) he was a prominent public figure, first in Calcutta and then in London, where he went in 1830 to plead the cause of the Moghul emperor. He supported English education and helped in the foundation of the Hindu College in 1816. He founded the first Bengali newspaper and started in Calcutta the first Indian printing press; he is the father of modern Bengali prose. He was an ardent advocate of social reform and a critic of *sati*, idolatry, and caste. In religion he was the founder of the Brahmo Samaj and author of *The Precepts of Jesus*. In politics he accepted the new liberal gospel and was in friendly contact with the Utilitarians. His many-sidedness betrayed no lack of depth, but rather the encyclopaedic and creative mind which appears but once in an age.

Ram Mohan Roy was a conservative in that he believed the Upanishads contained the essence of truth. He is often thought to have been an eclectic because he studied many religions and praised parts of them. In fact, he was a rationalist, who believed that Hinduism rested fundamentally upon reason and could face and, if necessary, appropriate all rational ideas from elsewhere. Like advocates of the central Catholic philosophy, he believed in authority because it was rational, not in reason because it was approved by authority. Reason, he said, was the guide of life. This principle once established as the heart of Hinduism, he could proceed both to prune current Hindu practices and to borrow from the West with a boldness and an assurance which went far beyond his own puzzled generation. He welcomed English education because it was the vehicle of Western ideas. He accepted democracy in its current liberal form (he gave a dinner to celebrate the July Revolution in France) as the political expression of the principle of personality which he found in Hindu thought. He welcomed Western science as reason applied to nature. He saw that once Hinduism relied upon its own rationalist philosophic outlook, its freedom from historical events or theological dogma made it less pervious to scientific criticism than any of the other religions. He could praise the Sermon on the Mount as an extension of the Gita's personal ethics.

In his day, Ram Mohan Roy was regarded as a marvel rather than a portent, as an occasional comet rather than as a rising sun. But the future justified his vision, and it gradually appeared that he had provided just that mixture of ideas which enabled the Hindus to face the West without losing their self-respect. Generations who probably never heard of Ram

Mohan Roy found that in following his path they lost the paralysing feeling that virtue had gone out of their faith. The kingdom of reason was within them after all. On this basis a Hindu could remain a Hindu though he were a reformer in a cautious way; he could accept Western political principles and so claim Western political privileges; he could study Western science without reserve and annex its results; he could use such of the Western material impedimenta as would give him material power; he could, in short, pick and choose without feeling that he was betraying himself or denying his past. Ram Mohan Roy reconciled Western modernism with Hindu honour.

Syed Ahmad Khan was born in 1817 of a family in Delhi with long traditions of Moghul service. After a classical Muslim education he took service with the British, and at the age of twenty-six published an authoritative account of the Delhi antiquities. For him the Mutiny was a dividing line which separated him for ever from the nodding greybeards of a fading court and the backward view of vain regrets. He spent the rest of his long life in promoting a synthetic and forward view among the discouraged Muslim community. His constructive achievement was the foundation of a Muslim College at Aligarh, now the Aligarh Muslim University. But, as with Ram Mohan Roy, it was the ideas which were important. In essence the Syed applied the same principle of reason to Islam as Ram Mohan Roy did to Hinduism. Whereas the Hindu reformer was faced with custom congealed into law, the Syed was confronted with a revelation cemented into a verbally inspired scripture reinforced by traditional interpretation. Syed Ahmad Khan accepted the fact of revelation and placed alongside it the principle of reason as its defender and interpreter. In this he was helped by the Greek tradition in Muslim thought; he used this and the new Western knowledge, much as did the Renaissance scholars, as a weapon both of authority and reason to break the crust of medieval scholasticism. Reason and nature were his oft-repeated watchwords. 'Reason alone is a sufficient guide' was a favourite saying, and in early days his followers were often called 'Naturis' or men of nature, which was later corrupted into Necheris.

On this basis the Syed launched a Muslim modernism which sought to reconcile traditional Islam with modern needs. He resisted the Wahabi advocacy of primitive Islam on the ground of reason; he countered European criticism of Muslim dogmatism by the new principle of inter-pretation, and of Muslim ethics (specially social ethics) by that of nature. Islamic law provided the everyday ethic for every believer, while Christ offered an ideal for superior spirits. Thus again, like Ram Mohan Roy, he drew the sting of Western criticism just where it pricked most tenderly. So fortified, he could proceed to borrow from the West as confidently as his Hindu prototype. Indeed, his task was easier, for Muslim and Western Christian share a common view of external phenomena. For both of them the world is real and the handiwork of God, for both of them men are God's creatures equal in his sight. The Syed was an enthusiastic advocate of Western science; it is significant that the first institution at Aligarh was a Scientific Society. He equally accepted Western democracy as an Islamic principle adapted to modern conditions. Western education followed inevitably in this evolution and found its Mecca in the foundation of Aligarh in 1875. All this led naturally to the birth of Muslim political consciousness. Here the Syed was cautious and never looked beyond self-government under British protection. He never ceased to co-operate with the British and sat in the Viceroy's Legislative Council during the last years of his life. But he was clear that there was a Muslim national consciousness quite distinct from the Hindu, and for that reason discouraged Muslims from any participation in the Indian National Congress on its formation in 1885. In his whole attitude was implicit the concept of Pakistan. It only needed the prospect of British withdrawal, something which in his day still seemed remote, to bring it to the surface.

Experience alone can show whether these parallel syntheses can stand the relentless logic of time. It is sufficient for our immediate purpose to note that they succeeded in convincing both thinking Hindus and Muslims that the new knowledge was not a deadly foreign bacillus threatening destruction to all they held dear, but a germicidal inoculation which might cause fever for a time, but would in the long run bring forth health and vigour.

12
The New India

CONSTITUTIONAL QUESTIONS have so dominated comment on India and the contemporary Indian consciousness itself, that they are apt to be regarded as the chief traces of Western influence. But as the previous chapters have attempted to show, the truth is far otherwise. The West has touched India at many points, and India has borrowed from the West in many ways. Above all, both Hindu and Muslim India (after a number of false starts) have worked out syntheses of East and West which have seemed to them satisfactory. They have at any rate enabled both Hindu and Muslim to look the West in the face once more and to reform their own cultures without a feeling of betrayal or surrender. We have now to note the growth of these syntheses, their stimuli, their method of articulation, their incarnation in political form, and their gradual weaving of the various cultural strands into a single political organization. Modern India, with its baffling mixture of Eastern revivalism and Western modernism, is the expression of these syntheses, and incessant public discussions are its apologetics as 'action is the ritual of contemplation and dialectic is its creed'.

It is one thing to construct a workable synthesis and another for it to take root and bear fruit. The seed must be scattered, the soil must be watered. How was it that the solution of a Bengali intellectual, which even he implied rather than proclaimed, became the working creed of the modern-minded Hindu? Part of the answer is that the conditions of the time favoured its spread, that the new ideas were carried over India by the wind of circumstance like feather-down on a summer breeze. But it is not enough to say that the thing happened. There are a number of factors which can be separately identified, and whose understanding gives important clues to the emergent new India of today.

First came the problem of publicity. In the early nineteenth century India possessed no modern publicity machine. The scattering of the seed had therefore to be incidental to other processes. The first vehicle of the new ideas was the system of Western education introduced by Lord William Bentinck. The study of English was already popular because of the opportunities it presented to the learner both in business and in official life. These opportunities were increased tenfold, and the study of English made virtually compulsory for all enterprising Indians, by its substitution for Persian as the official language and by its adoption for use in the higher law courts. Thus both the principal public professions of the law and government service demanded western studies, and the further linking of government service with a university degree sent every ambitious youth to the new colleges for regular courses of study. Here Western social, economic, and political ideas were imbibed and held in suspension, as it were, side by side with traditional concepts and ideas. All over India the same new ideas were broadcast, and the same ferment began. Along with the spread of English went the growth of the Press, the Indian-language Press as well as the English. The Press, which is still the main reading of the educated class, both broadcast the new ideas still further and related them to the traditional code. In the daily Press of nineteenth-century India can be studied the whole process of trial and error described in the last chapter and the gradual emergence of the Ram Mohan Roy solution as the accepted creed of the new India. A further aid to publicity was the habit of discussion and the cult of the lecture and public meeting, which is still one of the principal pleasures and occupations of the modern Indian. Then there was the agency of the government official. The prestige which all grades of officials enjoy provided a ready audience for their *obiter dicta*, and their ubiquity carried their ideas to remote areas where the Press did not penetrate. This applied especially, of course, to the Indian official. The Westerner was expected to be Western, but it was the Indian official on whose opinion others relied in seeking to borrow from the new without betraying the old. Finally may be listed the development of the local Indian languages which all entered upon a rapid period of development during the nine-teenth century. The distinguishing mark of this development was the rise of prose, and the medium for prose was the Indian-language Press and periodical literature. But whether in prose or in verse forms they were the languages understood by the man in the street, and therefore one of the best means of publicity.

The next problem is the growth of self-consciousness. How did the new synthesis develop into a definite movement and why did it finally assume a political form? The pressure of the West upon Indian society, the oppressive feeling of doubt and effeteness which it produced, has already been considered, but it is by no means clear why the movement for renewal should have taken the form of a campaign for self-government upon Western political lines. That there should be a desire for freedom from outside interference was as natural for the Hindu or Muslim as for the Englishman or American, but that independence of the West should take a Western form was by no means obvious. The answer is to be found in the nature of the forces, positive and negative, which were focused upon Indian society at the time.

The first of these was positive encouragement from the West. In the early years, British-Indian officials accepted and propagated the ideas of self-government on the basis of Indian acceptance of Western ideals. The attitude of such men as Elphinstone and Trevelyan had its effect upon their Indian contemporaries. The hook of the West, so to speak, was baited with the hope of independence. As the more generous school of Macaulay and Munro gave place to the Punjab school, and Dalhousie took the place of Bentinck; as the emphasis of Western freedom hardened in India into insistence on Western efficiency, encouragement by the British-Indian official was replaced by the encouragement of English writers and statesmen. Gladstone was prominent among these and through his friend Ripon made himself felt in India. The Queen's proclamation of 1858 was treasured as a gleam of hope in the apparently hopeless post-mutiny era. Kipling's *Paget, M.P.* was a caricature of the species from the angle of the efficiency school. The West encouraged India in another way also. The first burst of Sanskrit scholarship in the late eighteenth century, of which Sir William Jones was the leading figure, was followed after 1830 by the harvest of European Sanskrit and Pali studies centred round the French savant Burnouf and the German Max Müller. While Europeans in India were denigrating Indian civilization in all its aspects and counting it semi-barbarous, Western savants were discovering there fresh beauties and elegancies and plumbing fresh depths of thought. The Indians' belief in themselves was thus fortified from the very source of their doubt in themselves and sense of inadequacy. It was possible for a man to admire the West and to revere the East and to have European authority for both opinions. The hallmark of European approval, so to speak, was stamped on the Indo-European synthesis.

But great movements do not grow to maturity on approval; more often they thrive on opposition and some measure of discouragement. In India's case the rule held good. There was just enough hostility to stimulate, and not enough to crush. There was just enough power to awe, but not enough to overawe. There was just enough discomfort to create the will to break free, and not enough to paralyse it. First then there was the steady criticism of all Indian institutions, ideas, and customs. From the earnest hostility of the missionary, this passed through the chilly indifference of the official to the lofty disdain of the merchant. It is difficult to love the open despisers of your way of life, even if, and perhaps particularly if, you suspect privately they are partly in the right. European criticism acted as a steady stimulus of this new synthesis and a spur to Indian self-consciousness. Next came the slowly increasing discontent fostered by lack of opportunities to do the kind of work for which the new education had fitted the middle classes. The higher posts were virtually closed to Indians until nearly the end of the century, and for the lower ones there came to be a superabundance of candidates. It was inevitable that those affected should feel that all was not well in the state of India and should look to Western ways of justifying their discontent with conditions created by Western agencies. To the frustrated feeling of closed doors may be added the slowly deepening belief in the economic exploitation of India by Britain, which we have seen was the natural result of current ideas and practices. The imposition of a cotton excise in 1894, at the behest of Lancashire, was to India the symbol of this process. Then there was the widespread personal irritation, felt mainly by the growing middle class, arising from racial discrimination and the slights inflicted by a race-conscious minority of Europeans on a proud and sensitive people. It is well to remember that whereas in the eighteenth century claims of superiority tended to be based on the arguments of higher civilization and greater knowledge, in the nineteenth century they tended to be based on those of superior racial and inherent moral qualities. What was the man of reason's perquisite became the white man's burden. Distinctions on such a basis were far more galling to the victim because they arraigned not the system a man belonged to but the man himself. Finally, to all these stimulants may be added the love of power and independence inherent in all organized groups of human beings. The Muslims had a long tradition of empire and the Hindus a still older tradition and deeper desire for non-interference. The Arab Alberuni remarked in the eleventh century on the Hindu contempt for foreigners and his comment is typical of foreign commentators in general. The old form of independence was shown by the Mutiny to be impossible; there remained the new form of independence with Western forms to be attained by Western technique and an appeal to Western arguments. So the writings of Macaulay, Burke, and Mill with their hymns to liberty and praise of parliamentary democracy, which were prescribed as models of English prose, were remembered and treasured for their thought. The last triumph of the Whig school of politics was over the new middle class of mid-Victorian India.

These considerations help to explain why the growing self-consciousness of the new India eventually found a political mode of expression. But it was not its first or only form of expression, and it is well to note some of the other forms which it assumed. The earliest form was the discussion group among the Presidency town intellectuals, of which Ram Mohan Roy's Atmiya Sabha, or Society of the Soul, was the first important example. This was followed by clubs of all kinds, cultural, sporting, and social. As the middle class grew, professional associations grew with it. Bar associations sprang up in every town of India, to be centres of discussion and criticism, thorns in the flesh of local British officials, and spearheads of westernized political thought. Wherever the Bengali went, and he went nearly everywhere, he took his Bengali club with him. Medical associations, caste associations (through which cautious steps of social reform could be undertaken), and Chambers of Commerce appeared later. Later, social-reform bodies, partly inspired by and modelled upon missionary activities, sought to use Western philanthropic methods in the service of Indian regeneration. The chief of these was the Servants of India Society founded in Poona in 1905 by the great Gokhale, and the Poona Seva Sadan Society, which is devoted to the uplift of Indian women. All these activities sought in their various ways to reconcile the old and new by expressing Western ideas through Indian media or Indian ideas through Western forms.

The political articulation of the new India was thus the result of over fifty years of widespread cultural development. Like everything else in the new Indian synthesis, it was foreshadowed in the political activities of Ram Mohan Roy, and it was preceded by more than one false start before it finally started on a permanent course. As in so many other directions it was the joint stimuli of encouragement and distress which finally launched the Indian National Congress in 1885, and, of these, distress or indignation was perhaps the more potent because it touched feelings of pride and self-respect. The distress was caused by the controversy of 1884 over the Ilbert Bill, a measure which sought to make Europeans amenable to courts presided over by Indian judges. The fevered protests of race-conscious Europeans in Calcutta cut the sensitive new India to the quick and it seemed that, if the new ideas meant anything, some organized demonstration was required. Encouragement came from liberal opinion in England, which made itself felt through Dadabhai Naoroji, the Bombay Parsi (who for some years was a Liberal Member of Parliament), through Lord Ripon, in a lofty and guarded way through the new Viceroy, Lord Dufferin, and through a small number of liberal-minded Englishmen in India itself. The chief of these were A. O. Hume and Sir William Wedderburn, both retired civil servants, the latter of whom was twice President of Congress. But though indignation was the spur to action, respect and moderation were the keynotes of the speeches. The delegates were as yet too dazzled by the glare of the British imperial sun to think of such a thing as separation; gratitude for past favours received was more strongly felt than discontent at benefits denied. The theme-song was of new horizons and of freedom revealed, rather than of avenues to liberty blocked. Progress was to be along Western lines within the existing framework. Even in 1905 Gokhale could, in the foundation deed of the Servants of India Society, accept British rule in India as under 'the inscrutable dispensation of Providence'. In 1885 it was not even inscrutable.

Founded in this modest and deprecatory way, the Congress at first represented only a few individuals in the whole mass of the new India. But its ideas were so clearly implicit in the whole attitude of the new India to the West that its progress was remarkably rapid. The cloud no bigger than a man's hand lengthened in its shadow over the whole of India and Indian life in sixty years. The progress was on two fronts, the political and the cultural. Politically it developed from a cautious debating society into a national society on one-party and authoritarian lines, and culturally it influenced and embraced one by one all the chief classes of Hindu society and monopolized all the chief means of social expression. Broadly speaking, Congress became both the cultural and the political voice of the new Hindu India. The battles of opinion were fought out within its ranks, the stresses of interest were within rather than outside. Thus, back-to-the-village neo-Hinduism as personified by Gandhi, Western democracy and secularism in the person of Nehru, the party boss and militant Hindu in the person of Patel, and the Brahminized Gladstonian Liberal in the person of Rajagopalachari, were all to be found within its ranks. Only the extreme orthodox who rejected the West, and the Communists who rejected the East, remained outside. And they were rightly outside, because they both rejected the synthesis to which the new India had given her allegiance.

In the political growth of Congress we can trace stages in the technique of action, in outlook, and ultimate aim. These again were influenced by developments which went on both within and without India. At first the sessions of the Congress were no more than the annual meetings of a large-scale debating society. The accepted mode of procedure was formal speeches followed by resolutions asking for detailed improvements and moderate reforms. Under men like Gokhale it seemed to be heading straight for the decorous haven of a Victorian parliamentary system. From about 1905, when Lord Curzon's Bengal Partition stirred angry feelings, public agitation was undertaken by Congress. Public meetings and Press campaigns were organized, and demands became more strident and far-reaching. The Morley-Minto reforms of 1909 brought about a short honeymoon between the Congress led by Gokhale and the Government of Lord Hardinge. But the first World War heralded a change. The stresses created by that war renewed tension which the Congress naturally exploited. Control passed to the extremist Tilak and then to his greater successor, Gandhi. Gandhi both widened the appeal of Congress by appealing to the peasant masses as well as the middle classes and changed its tactics by introducing revolutionary methods. He won the Hindu masses by assuming the attributes of a Hindu saint—poverty, ascetism, and devotion—and he kept hold of the intellectuals by talking and acting like a Western-trained lawyer. His position in the synthesis may be described as right-centre. His combination of Western and Hindu characteristics enabled both conservative and radical, simple Hindus and bustling Westerners, to see in him a safe guide to freedom on Western lines and to modernization without sacrifice of ancient ideals. His services were therefore of incalculable value; his work transformed Congress from a Western political body into a national cultural one, embracing elements from both East and West. And this he did in spite of an expressed opposition to Western 'materialism' and its expression in modern industry. He mulcted the mill-owners while advocating hand spinning, upheld the dignity of Hinduism while attacking the outcaste system, and popularized Western inventions like the radio and modern hygiene while condemning Western science. It was an extraordinary tactical *tour de force*. He introduced and made effective the characteristically Western weapon of revolutionary action and he gave this action a characteristically Indian form. This was the principle of *ahimsa* or non-violence (influenced, it is true, by Tolstoy's ideas) which was expressed in the system of non-violent non-co-operation with, or later, non-violent civil disobedience to government. In successive campaigns he perfected the technique and increased its force by multiplying the number of its practitioners, so that while each effort ended formally in failure, the Congress always emerged stronger than before. By 1942 Congress could threaten the existence of the Government at the height of a war and when backed by more than a million troops.

Along with a development of tactics went a widening of aim and scope. At first the aim was a modest hope of a share in the direction of government and the process of legislation. The first World War, when the British Empire was visibly embarrassed, and even when it finally emerged victorious was clearly no longer the invincible leviathan it had formerly appeared to be, brought about a radical change. The aim was now self-government within the Empire, presently adapted to the new conception of Dominion Status, and this continued in essence until the second World War, in spite of the formal adoption of independence as the professed political objective in 1929.

During the thirties another profound change overtook the Congress leaders. Hitherto they had thought in terms of concessions from an irremovable British government. But now, especially after the great 1935 Act had begun to work and revealed the extent to which the British grip was weakening, the leaders' thoughts began to turn to what was to come after the British. Concession politics were transmuted by almost insensible degrees into power politics. By the late thirties the Congress was thinking, not merely of getting rid of the British, but of controlling the India which would be left to them. Here the Muslims came in, and henceforward Congress was fighting on two fronts. Every move was dictated by the wish not only to expel the British, but to succeed them in the sole control of the country. We shall return to the Muslims a little later and here be content with noting the beginning of the political process which led straight to the eventual Indian partition.

We may now trace the extension of Congress influence over the various departments of the national life. As the Hindu-British synthesis led inevitably, as it developed, to political consciousness and so to a political national movement, so the political Congress, as it developed, absorbed within itself or took successively under its wing, the various Hindu groups within the country and the various cultural activities which had marked the national revival. Congress may be said to have completed its control of the new middle classes in the age of Gokhale and Tilak. Gandhi and his western Indian lieutenant, Vallabhbhai Patel, extended their influence to the peasants by the political devices of no-rent and no-tax campaigns and by the Hindu devices of asceticism and renunciation. The new capitalist classes, themselves of course Western-educated, were won by support for their interests in the name of economic nationalism. So the extraordinary spectacle was seen of wealthy mill-owners, whose money was the product of Western machinery and Western technique based on Western science, themselves wearing home-spun cloth in honour of Gandhi and subscribing heavily to propaganda avowedly directed against their whole industry. Nor were the new industrial classes neglected. Congressmen or Congress sympathizers were active in this field also, though a good deal of their thunder was stolen by the more radical and thorough-going Communists. Not even reverence for Gandhi and the cult for soul-force could altogether bridge the gulf between the unlimited profits of the mill-owner and the unlimited wage demands of the Communist agitator.

A harder task confronted the Congress in the States, and success in this field would perhaps put the seal on the reality of the Hindu-British (or European) synthesis as the working creed of modern India. For long the States seemed impervious to the charmings of either democrats or nationalists, and Congress wavered between the backwater theory, acquiescence, and threats of complete abolition. After 1920, however, a marked change came over the mental atmosphere of the States. The attitude of blunt conservatism gave place slowly after 1857 to a princely edition of the synthesis, which may be described as enlightened despotism tempered by Western ideals. The best Princes were enlightened despots in the eighteenth-century manner, the worst, idlers in the Parisian mode or palace monsters in the Renaissance style. From 1920 the Congress instrument in the States was the States Peoples Conference; there was a steady and perceptibly quickening development from the idea of progress from above to the idea of progress in partnership, from enlightened despotism to constitutional monarchy. The last of the classes to be touched politically or culturally were the old landed upper classes. For long they held aloof from modern education and public life, but they are now moving in the opposite direction to that of the middle class. The middle class proceeded from Western education to Western political ideas and demands for power. The upper classes now see the seats of power opening to all comers and are seeking Western education to fit themselves for it. And as Congress is the chief avenue to power even when it fulminates against landlords, an increasing number of the old families are attaching themselves to it.

The same process took place in the cultural and social manifestations of the synthesis. Every cultural activity, such as organizations of painters

or writers, tended to develop Congress sympathies, and Congress in its
turn tended to bring all such activities within its influence. Two examples
must suffice to illustrate the process. The women's movement was
obviously inspired by Western ideals. It was taken up by Hindus themselves and justified on Hindu grounds. Its organization was at first non-
political, but then the All-India Women's Conference, whether or not it
was formally affiliated to the Congress, became in practice the women's
side of the movement. For it, in recent years, the political question was
more important than anything else. A similar development took place
in the matter of the Untouchables. The original impulse to raise them
came from Western missionary sources. Hindus accepted the demand
and justified it on Hindu grounds. Societies were formed and work
commenced. Then came Mr. Gandhi with his Harijan movement and
the whole social-uplift movement, an expression of Western humanitarianism and egalitarian principles, was baptized as it were into Hinduism and confirmed into the Congress fold. Congress is not the only social
agency, but it is certainly the chief, and it is now accepted that Congress
and so the new India stands for social betterment.

It is now time to return to the Muslims. Where do they stand in the
development of the new synthesis? If the foregoing argument is correct,
the Muslims should have developed their own synthesis on parallel but
distinct lines. This is, in fact, what happened, though more recently and
less completely than in the case of the Hindus. It should always be
remembered that the bulk of Muslim India, in the Punjab and North-
West, came under British influence at least a generation later (and often
much more) than the rest of India. In general Muslim progress towards
an Anglo-Islamic synthesis lagged a good generation behind that of the
Anglo-Hindu, both because the starting-point was later, and also because
the progress of education was less rapid. There were two other factors
retarding the process. Muslims preferred British to Hindu or Sikh rule,
and therefore were slower to react against it; they felt the weight of the
Western challenge less keenly because they possessed more of the Western
outlook in their own tradition. But while these considerations made them
later off the mark at the outset, they tended to hasten the process when
it was Hindu rule which threatened and the irritation of Western rule
was withdrawn.

The Anglo-Islamic synthesis was worked out by Sir Syed Ahmad Khan
in the seventies and eighties of the last century, and was propagated
through Aligarh from 1875 onwards. But it was only from 1921 that
large-scale education was developed in the Punjab. If Hindus and

Muslims both tried to work out a synthesis between their respective cultures and the challenging ideas of the West, it followed that, the two cultures being radically different in the first place, the resulting chemical compounds must be different also. This is in fact what happened. The first concrete sign of divergence was the Syed's refusal to join the National Congress on its foundation in 1885. The next was the formation of the Muslim League in 1906 in response to the Hindu agitation for the partition of Bengal. The third was the insistence on communal or separate electorates in the Morley-Minto reforms of 1909. What was thought to be a concession to foolish though intelligible fears in 1909 became a regrettable concession to prejudice in 1919 and an accepted constitutional principle in 1935. From the time of the formation of the Muslim League the vitality of Muslim separatism was in direct proportion to the militancy of Hinduism. The threat to Turkey in the first World War brought Hinduism and Islam into temporary alliance in the post-war years; the beginnings of serious self-government saw them draw apart in mutual suspicion; full provincial autonomy in 1937 and a Congress drive to absorb the League saw the League revivified and united under the one-time nationalist Jinnah. From this stage to the formal demand for Pakistan[1] was but a logical step which the Congress did no more than hasten. Jinnah was not really inconsistent; he only realized that Indian Islam was a cultural unit separate from Hinduism, that the Anglo-Islamic synthesis was therefore distinct from the Hindu-British synthesis, and that each must in consequence seek a separate political as well as cultural expression.

By logical process, step by step, both Hinduism and Islam built up a system of life and thought which endeavoured to absorb Western ideals without abandoning their own. The West expressing itself characteristically in political forms, these new approximations to the West necessarily did so too. As they were different in origin, they varied in their transformation and expressed themselves in separate though partly similar political forms. It is only when the cultural difference has been expressed politically that each side can cease to emphasize the differences rather than the likenesses, and that a sense of common interest can begin to build a bridge across the gulf which logical necessity has created.

[1] The word was invented by Choudhri Rahmat Ali and first published by him in his pamphlet *Now or Never* (1933).

13
India Under Nehru

ALMOST FROM THE MOMENT OF INDEPENDENCE the new Union was placed under grave stress. Apart from the shock of partition there was the brutal upheaval which followed in the Punjab. A predisposing cause was the communal tension which had been mounting ever since the conclusion of the war and had already led to grave outbreaks of disorder in Calcutta and Bihar. Wherever populations were mixed, fear was uppermost and violence a constant threat. Immediate causes were a virtual Muslim League revolt in the Punjab, when excluded from power on the fall of the Khizr ministry early in 1947, and the determination of the Sikhs not to be divided by an artificial political boundary drawn to meet the demands of others. The actual boundary award, which was published just after partition, confirmed their worst fears, and the die of violence was cast. The boundary force proved quite unequal to its task. What followed was not so much a revolt as a war of extermination. No useful purpose can be achieved by trying to weigh the balance and apportion blame; it is sufficient to say that half a million lives are thought to have been lost and some twelve million people involved in painful and often pitiable migration. For a time authority ceased from the Beas to the Jumna and was threatened in Delhi itself. Both countries found added to their existing problems feeling of great bitterness on their mutual frontier and large-scale social dislocation. In Pakistan the problem was perhaps more pressing, because a larger proportion of its people and land was directly affected. But in India the area of the upheaval was close to the capital itself, and no Delhi government could be unmoved by the passion which surrounded it. In both countries, therefore, the storm left behind it a ground swell of resentment which it must take many years of political and social calm to still. It will now be convenient to trace briefly the fortunes of each country in turn and to note their handling of the issues which confronted them.

In India the first few months were dominated by the after-effects of the Punjab storm. The cry of the dispossessed for revenge was loud and was swelled by extremist Hindu groups. An easy target for such feelings was available in the surviving Muslims of Delhi. It was Mahatma Gandhi's intervention on their behalf, and particularly to rescue the mosques of Delhi from refugee occupation,[1] that led to his death in January 1948 at the hand of a Hindu extremist. The horror inspired by this deed set in motion a reaction which drained away support from the extremist groups. The apparent revival marked by the election of Mr. Purshotamdas Tandon to the Congress Presidency in 1950 ended with his enforced retirement from office less than a year later, and the extent of the revulsion was revealed in the election results of 1951–2. Extremism countered, the task of resettlement remained. This the Government attacked energetically, both in the Punjab and the Delhi region. Though fewer refugees came in than went out, many of them were townsmen, while the survivors in the East Punjab had taken some of the vacant land. In consequence the East Punjab could not hold them all. This accounted for the large numbers who drifted to Delhi and beyond, and whom the Government were for some time compelled to feed *gratis* as a precautionary measure. Suburban extensions were pushed forward and satellite towns, of which that at Faridabad was the most striking, were developed. After five years the problem, if not solved, was at any rate under control. A further problem was presented by the presence of a compact Sikh body, over four millions strong, in the East Punjab. The Sikhs were prevented from attaining their goal of statehood within the Indian Union partly by their own divisions. On a long-term basis there would seem to be some ground for the belief that the age-old absorptive power of Hinduism may exercise its fascination, affiliating the Sikhs to itself as a martial frontier caste. On the short-term, the extremist Akalis failed to achieve much success at the elections.

The first shock of partition survived and absorbed, the Government could turn its attention to the several major problems which faced the new state. Foremost among these was the question of prestige and, linked with it, that of the Princely States. Any new state must convince its citizens of its determination and ability to rule, and in a country so large and containing so many divergent interests this was particularly

[1] One hundred and eighteen mosques were evacuated as a condition of his giving up his fast.

important. The shocks which accompanied partition made such an assertion not only urgent but vital. A prerequisite of the necessary action was unity within the Government. In the autumn of 1947, there were signs of tension within the controlling group of the Congress itself. Gandhi, Nehru, and Patel all seemed to some extent to be pursuing different policies. Gandhi's death brought the two tendencies of tolerant secular democracy and intolerant militant Hinduism face to face; the prospect of ruin precipitated a solution of compromise which lasted for the period of Patel's life. While Nehru controlled foreign affairs, Parliament, and constitution-making, he refrained from applying his socialist convictions to big business; Patel continued his party and industrial management but curbed his Hindu ardour in the interests of secular democracy and to some extent disciplined his capitalist associates in the name of the welfare state. Both men realized that neither could govern for long without the other, and both were realistic enough to make and to maintain substantial concessions to the other's point of view. Order was restored and maintained with vigour against extremists at both ends. Gandhi's assassin was executed after a full trial on the one side, and Communist agitators detained without trial and their organizations broken up on the other.

Sardar Vallabhbhai Patel at once took in hand the integration of the Princely States with the rest of India. Most of the Princes, after a characteristic last-minute attempt to form an independent bloc or 'Third Force' of their own, accepted the inevitable and acceded to the Indian Union. But it is doubtful if many of them realized the fate which awaited them. Their property and to some extent their dignity were saved at the price of their power. They were treated like German imperial princes by Napoleon; while retaining their princely rank, their authority was mediatized and their States thrown together to form larger unions over which one of their number presided with the archaic title of Rajpramukh. In the course of months the 562 States of British India dwindled to ten 'Part B' States, of whom only two ultimately retained their previous identity, and three 'Part C' States. Many were absorbed in adjacent provinces, as Baroda in Bombay, Pudukottah in Madras, and the Orissa States in Orissa. The Rajput States became the new State of Rajasthan, Indore and Gwalior were merged into Madhya Bharat, the Sikh Punjab States into the Patiala and Punjab States Union. The Gujarat State revived the ancient name of Saurashtra, certain Central Indian States became Vindhya Pradesh, and the Simla hill States Himachal Pradesh, while Travancore and Cochin were amalgamated.

The only State which maintained a precarious independence for a time was Hyderabad, but when persuasion failed it was incorporated in the Union by the 'police action' of September 1948. Much skill as well as firmness and some ruthlessness was displayed by the Sardar.

So matters rested until the general States reorganization of 1956. Then Hyderabad disappeared altogether, divided between Telugu-speaking Andhra and Bombay, Travancore-Cochin was merged into the new Malabar (Malayali-speaking) State of Kerala, while Mysore, enlarged to be the Kannada-speaking State, lost its Rajpramukh and was so changed in shape as to be hardly recognizable. The Punjab States were merged with the East Punjab. Shortly after the Bombay State was divided into the two States of Maharashtra and Gujarat, which in turn absorbed the former princely lands included in Saurashtra.

The influence of Pandit Nehru can be largely seen in the framing of the new constitution. This was the work of the Constituent Assembly which had been elected by the provincial assemblies as the result of the elections of 1946. The first feature of the new constitution which the observer will notice is that of continuity. The constitution of 1935 was not in fact set aside or revised, but expanded and developed along the lines which it had itself anticipated. The principle of parliamentary government which had been established in the provinces and fore-shadowed at the centre, was fully implemented. The working head of the Government was the Prime Minister, who succeeded to most of the Viceroy's prerogatives, and a constitutional sovereign appeared in the person first of the Governor-General and then of the President of the Republic. The most striking examples of continuity were perhaps the re-tention of the power of legislation by temporary decree and the power to detain, without trial, in the interests of public safety. Once executive power was in the hands of Indians and the Government was responsible to an elected assembly the old arguments for executive and legal 'safeguards' appealed with new force to the Congress leaders. The federal principle was retained though additional emphasis was laid upon the federal power. What the provinces gained in dignity by the conferment of the new title of 'states' they lost in autonomy by the expansion of federal authority. Here again the Congress leaders now found themselves in agreement with their predecessors on the need for a strong centre. Finally, the rule of law continued its sway unchallenged, being strengthened by a declaration of fundamental rights and buttressed by the Federal Court of Appeal.

The principle of continuity was not really affected by the new features of the constitution except in two respects. The strengthening of the

central authority was no departure in principle but rather a fresh emphasis on a principle always stressed by the British. A declaration of fundamental rights was certainly something new, recalling American and
continental precedents rather than British. But it was essentially an
underlining of the British-inspired rule of law, one of the British importations which had been generally appreciated and which had struck
the deepest roots in India. In the matter of representation it is clear that
the central House of the People (Lok Sabha) and House of States (Rajan
Sabha) are essentially the old Assembly and Council of State writ large,
as are also the various States legislatures. The two departures from the
past were the introduction of universal suffrage, thus raising the electorate at a stroke from thirty to a hundred and seventy-five millions, and
the virtual abolition of Princely India. The first of these was a bold and
radical measure, but it was only an extension of the logic of the 1935
Act, which had itself increased the provincial franchise fivehold. The
absorption of Princely India thus stands out as the one revolutionary
change in the constitution. The recognition of the Princes was com-
plimentary, their place in the constitution was vestigial and in no way
organic. Since 1956 they have virtually disappeared from the Indian
political scene.

No recognition was given to the Hindu religion and no place found for
its luminaries. Caste was declared to have no legal force and untouchability to be abolished. The new state is secular in tone and neutral in
religion, thus conforming once more to the practice of its predecessors.
Thus independence saw no return towards the past, but rather a
quickened step towards the modern West. It is surely significant that the
one revolutionary move was aimed at Indian tradition itself, and the main
references to Indian institutions were critical.

Nehru and Patel worked together until Patel's death in December 1950.
But they were not easy bedfellows. Patel was one of the founding fathers
and as the veteran organizer of the Congress party considered that he had
a better title to the premiership. Shortly before his death he secured the
election as Congress President of the orthodox and right-wing Purshotamdas Tandon. Some months later Tandon challenged Nehru's independent authority as Premier; a short struggle ensued ending, as with
Bose's challenge to Gandhi, in Tandon's disappearance. This was more
than a personal struggle; by demonstrating Nehru's indispensability to
Congress, it marked the beginning of his personal reign as ruler of India.

To the outside world, Nehru's position seemed to be stronger than that
of any other national leader at that time. He controlled a party with a

large parliamentary majority which, with the mystique of Gandhi and the achievement of independence behind it, seemed immovably fixed in power. He himself, as the chosen heir of Gandhi, was regarded as the last of the founding fathers and increasingly as the father of the nation. To the party ascendancy and public esteem almost amounting to worship he added a rich and colourful personality which enabled him easily to dominate his colleagues in cabinet and party, to hypnotize the middle classes with his speeches, and to dazzle the people with his mass meetings. His abounding vitality carried him to the four corners of India and enabled him to make innumerable speeches. His interests ranged from hill trekking to cricket and helicopters. The trim figure in neat *achkan* marked with a single rose and the swinging silver-topped cane, vibrant with nervous energy and its concomitant impatience, flitted everywhere, inspiring, exhorting, upbraiding. People said that the new India had found its Akbar.

But there were hidden limitations to this apparently irresistible figure. His hold on the party was not as complete as it appeared to be on the surface. Before independence the Congress was a national body constituting in effect a one-party state. It contained elements from right to left of the political spectrum, united under the Gandhian umbrella in the name of nationalism. The only public future lay with the party, so that people of all shades of opinion joined it on the plea of patriotism. This magic worked so long as independence was the issue, but thereafter there was inevitably divergence of opinion as to the correct policy to follow. Nehru's prestige was too great for anyone to hope to set up a successful opposition. Those who distrusted or disapproved of his views therefore, for the most part, stayed within the Congress and opposed from within. The defeat of Tandon prevented them from using the party machine to check or harass the Premier. They therefore went underground and sought to achieve by obstruction what they feared to attempt by open opposition. During his years of power Nehru's real opponents were not Communists, Socialists, or avowed communalists, but those of his own house professing to be his supporters. They provided a deadweight of opposition which was much stronger than most outside observers realized.

The second limitation came from his own personality. With all his intelligence, fire, and vision, Nehru somewhat lacked a certain decisiveness, the knack of getting things done, of pushing things to conclusions. His commanding personality confounded those who sought to oppose him in cabinet or in public, but he had not the art of working easily with equals or attracting a school of followers. As veterans like Maulana Azad and Pandit Pant dropped away it was noticed that their places were taken by lesser men who would not say 'no' in private or act positively in public. There was no Nehru political school as there had been of William Pitt or Sir Robert Peel. No lesser tree could grow beneath the parent shade. Nehru was too impatient of detail to be a good administrator and too dominating a character to compensate for this by delegating authority. So decisions taken at the top were often quietly sabotaged by those who had publicly agreed to them or simply failed to find implementation through lack of instructed subordinates who could transmit the original impetus to the end product. Nehru felt a need for support and counsel though he was stiffly independent in public. In early days it was his masterful father Motilal to whom he deferred and with whom he argued. Later and for many years it was Gandhi from whom he only finally emancipated himself on the eve of independence. In his earlier years of power after Patel's death he had Pandit Pant for home and G. S. Bajpai for external affairs. Then came Krishna Menon, a fellow-intellectual and dedicated left-wing Congressman. He spoke a language that Nehru understood, he provided a sounding-board for his ideas, and he exercised an influence second only to that of Gandhi. Nehru was the intellectual's delight, with his freedom from tradition, his soliloquies and speculations, his rationalism, his doubts, and his literary dilettantism. But he had also the intellectual's infirmity, an inability to make firm decisions. Like Hamlet, it was constantly for him 'to be or not to be' and his projects, like Hamlet's, too often 'with this regard, their currents turned awry and lost the name of action'.

Nehru's views were those of a democratic socialist who was also an ardent nationalist. He developed these views in the twenties as a young man, while at the same time resiling from Russian Communism which he regarded as harshly authoritarian. The events of the thirties, with Stalin's purges and the world depression, confirmed both these views. Democracy for him meant personal rights and the liberty of self-government, which for him took a parliamentary form. Beyond all this he was profoundly moved by the spectacle of Indian poverty, a sentiment first induced by his contact with the *kisans* or peasants of his home region around Allahabad during the first non-cooperation campaign in 1921 and confirmed by his later tours throughout India. With such ideas there was obviously much to be done in the then condition of India and there was also bound to be much opposition from vested interests.

We can now observe the shape of Nehru's India. He began by alarming

Indian and foreign capitalists, but he soon realized that he could not do without them. After all Indian big business had been and still was a heavy backer of Congress. He settled down to the ideas of a socialist controlled rather than a socialist society. Liberal principles were to be implemented in such fields as education, welfare, and personal rights, while the state exercised an overall control of the economy. Industry was divided into public and private sectors, the state retaining for itself all large-scale developments of national import. Existing private concerns operating in what was to be the public sector, like Tatas, were left alone. The calculation was that the development intended in this sector would so escalate the state share of big industry as to reduce the existing private concerns to comparative unimportance. The turning-point in India's economic development came with the setting up of a Planning Commission in 1950 which has produced a series of five-year plans. It coincided with the launching of the Colombo Plan which provided valuable initial aid. The Planning Commission was Nehru's instrument for attacking the problem of poverty which so oppressed him. Industry would provide jobs for the unemployed and new mouths, and its production would gradually raise the general standard of living. India would become, like Russia, a country with a mixed economy of balanced agricultural and industrial elements with overall state control. The first five-year plan had an agricultural bias and was considered successful. It was claimed that the national income rose 18 per cent during the period. The second plan was much more ambitious, aiming at a twenty-five per cent increase in the national income and involving a total outlay of five thousand million pounds and the raising of two thousand million of these pounds by loans. The emphasis this time was on industry and it is from this time that India's great steel plants, built by Britain, Russia, and Germany, date. The third five-year plan was even more ambitious. The total outlay envisaged was nearly eight thousand million pounds of which nearly five was to go to the public sector. The plan involved external assistance of two and a half thousand millions, the alternative being deficit finance or inflation. The plan is now in its closing stages and it is clear that while it has solid achievements to its credit it will not attain its targets. A re-appraisal is proceeding in the course of framing a fourth plan. It must be said in general of this great effort to banish dire poverty and unemployment that it has not succeeded in its major objectives, in spite of very positive achievements. These achievements are, in the technical sphere, the provision of a modern industrial potential within the Indian state. Industrial production rose by 50 per cent in the eight years 1951–9; in addition to the steel industry which now produces more than six million tons a year the aluminium and cement industries have been greatly expanded, and the machine tool, diesel, steam and electric engine, automobile, and fertilizer industries virtually created. India can supply her basic industrial needs, though not her basic raw materials. To service and feed these industries the middle class has undergone a great expansion as can be seen by the expansion in any of India's great cities. Having said so much we come to the limitations of the effort. The national product grew largely in the Nehru régime but the *per capita* income much less so. In spite of this increase the *per capita* income is still no more than £22 10s. 0d. a year or Rs. 300. This means that the new middle class has absorbed most of this increased national income and even their average *per capita* income is barely £50 a year. The rural population still constitutes eighty per cent of the total, so that apart from the villages on the edge of great cities which can profit by supplying their needs, and enterprising States like the Punjab and Madras, it can be said that their position is largely unchanged. Towards the end of the period a warning signal appeared in the rise of prices. During the fifties they remained fairly stable, but by 1961 they had risen nearly twenty per cent and since then by another twenty. The rise in food prices has been proportionately greater. Another disappointment has been the failure to attain the food production target of a hundred million tons of foodgrains. Production reached eighty-one million tons in 1961 but has since veered round the eighty mark. As a consequence shipments of grain continued to be heavy, adding the elements of uncertainty and additional outlay of exchange to the already perplexing situation.

A fundamental factor in this disappointing result was the increase of population. The population was expected by the planners to be about four hundred and eight millions in 1961 instead of which it was four hundred and thirty-nine millions. In 1965 it was estimated at four hundred and sixty-five millions with an annual increase of nearly eight millions a year. This avalanche of new mouths has more than swallowed up all the increase in food production. In the years 1961–2 to 1963–4 there was no material gain in *per capita* income, in spite of the large industrial expansion, mainly for this reason. Nehru was well aware of this process and its dangers and he set on foot birth-control measures. But he was unable to arouse the articulate public, which itself practises birth control, to a sense of urgency in spreading it to the masses.

Nehru's liberal principles led him to support education. The largest democratic electorate in the world should not be illiterate. The expansion already taking place was intensified. In the higher reaches the results were striking. By Nehru's death the twenty universities of pre-independence India had become sixty-two for India alone. Technical universities on the American model were included, and so were the higher research establishments including an atomic energy plant. The emphasis was on science; while the migration of students to Britain and America continued on a large scale it was clear that India was fast heading towards the provision of her own technical corps to sustain the apparatus of a modernized society. In elementary education the result was not so impressive. While in some of the great cities like Delhi primary education was virtually universal, in the lesser towns and the countryside it lagged behind. The middle classes were not enthusiastic about a literate proletariat and Nehru was not able to impart the necessary drive for achieving it. At the time of his death the literacy rate was twenty-four per cent, with the proportion of men to women of two to one.

Nehru's feeling for personal rights in a secular society led him to action in two further directions. In the sphere of personal rights there was an attack on the great estate-holders or *zamindars*, particularly in Bengal, Bihar, and parts of Uttar Pradesh. This had long been an item on the Congress programme, though enthusiasm seemed to grow less as the hour of action approached. The landed interests had, in fact, a foot in the Congress camp and they used their position to the full. Nehru persevered to the extent of amending the constitution but the terms of compensation were generous enough for it to be contended that the cultivators actually experienced little relief. A major problem, of the division of holdings and the multiplying landless labourers, remained. The new industries were to find them jobs, and so they were drawn into the towns there to become the new shanty-town and pavement-dwelling proletariat. A more encouraging expression of the democratic principle was the extensive encouragement of village *panchayats* or committees. The importance of these bodies had been recognized by the early British administrators but they had languished until a revival movement began in the twenties. The new Government extended them and made them an integral part of local government. Various judgements have been passed on *panchayati raj*. It may be said that the long-term effect of a measure on so large a scale cannot be determined in the course of a few years. That there are lights and shades in the programme there is no doubt, but on balance one can regard it as a measure of great significance, not so much for its revival of a traditional governmental technique, as for its importance in promoting democratic processes at the grass roots of society. At present *panchayats* may be the organs of local aspirations and politics, but when there is general education in the villages they may become the essential vehicles of mass democracy.

The liberal idea of personal rights ran directly counter to essential portions of Hindu law, still largely based on the ancient Laws of Manu. There was a widespread desire for some amelioration of these laws but there was also stout orthodox opposition. Nehru at first optimistically thought that he could pass the necessary legislation in a single session but when he found that the opposition, largely from within his own party, was both obstinate and resourceful, he persevered with greater determination than perhaps he showed on any other issue. The controversy largely turned on the rights of women which traditional Hindu law severely restricted. Nehru, whose family had long been secular in the Western sense with a strong belief in personal rights, and whose sister, Mrs. Pandit, and daughter, Indira, have been important public figures, believed that India's progress largely depended on the advancement of her women and that this could only be secured by defining their rights in law. It took six years to pass the two principal bills[1] covering this subject. The new laws, of which at present only the educated minority can actually avail themselves, do mark an epoch in the development of Hindu society. Polygamy, which though rarely practised outside princely families was recognized in traditional law, has been finally abolished; women receive equal rights of inheritance with men, divorce within Hindu society is introduced, and there are legal provisions for the maintenance of widows and separated wives. While the new laws can only be used at present by those who know about them and can go to court, they may in the course of time lead to major changes in Indian society. This, rather than his more spectacular political or economic achievements, may eventually come to be Jawaharlal Nehru's major claim to posthumous fame.

It was in overseas affairs that Nehru at first appeared to achieve his greatest success and finally suffered his heaviest reverse. His control here was more complete than anywhere else owing to lack both of knowledge and expertise among politicians and administrators, and of interest among the public. Indian relations with Britain had first to be considered. The immediate transition was smoothed by the continuance of Lord Mountbatten as the first Governor-General of the new India. His tact and geniality proved invaluable in convincing the new rulers of the determination of Britain to accept the new order and indulge in no back-

[1] The Hindu Succession Act (1955) and the Hindu Marriage Act (1956).

ward-looking glances. The more they became convinced of this, the less anxious were they to cut loose from the Commonwealth. But there survived a volume of feeling which found in even nominal attachment to another state some derogation of national self-respect. India was too great to be even apparently subordinate to a foreign ruler. A solution was found by which India became a republic (on 26 January 1950) while remaining a member of the Commonwealth and recognizing the Crown as the head of the latter. This arrangement has been found workable in practice as well as convenient in theory. It survived the strain of the Suez crisis and was vigorously championed by Mr. Nehru, both during the Russian visitation and in the domestic durbar of the Lok Sabha.

With Pakistan a solution was not easy. The Punjab massacres exacerbated feeling and then came the Kashmir problem. The Maharajah's accession to India was provoked by an incursion of frontier Pathans; Indian intervention in its turn increased resistance from the Muslims of Poonch, who were backed by Pakistan. The deadlock in Kashmir has lasted since then. It proved a serious drain on Indian resources and an embarrassment in her bid for influence elsewhere, for to the realist's question, 'How many divisions?' the answer was 'They are in Kashmir.' Mr. Nehru throughout protested his determination not to settle the question by force and at first added willingness to accept the results of a plebiscite. But no proposals of the United Nations for arranging such a vote proved acceptable to him. His attitude in the matter gradually hardened. He allowed his friend Sheikh Abdullah to be forcibly replaced and detained by the more pro-Indian Bakshi Ghulam Muhammad; at the beginning of 1957 he accepted the Kashmir Assembly's declaration of union with India and regarded the question as closed.

In some other respects India and Pakistan gradually sorted out their problems. The complicated refugee property question was largely settled or at least closed after years of disputation. The question of the canal headwaters in the Punjab was the most dangerous of all. India held the headwaters of the Punjab canals and could therefore precipitate a crisis at a moment's notice. Her announcement of her intention, in connection with the great Bhakra dam project, to absorb all the Sutlej water which had hitherto filled several Pakistan canals, made the situation still more delicate. This problem was at length solved in 1960 through the efforts of the World Bank. It was agreed that India should take the water of the three eastern rivers, the Sutlej, Beas, and Ravi, while Pakistan took that of the three western ones, the Chenab, Jhelum, and Indus. To offset the loss of water by Pakistan from Indian use of the three western rivers, the

Bank financed a scheme for constructing transverse channels by which the eastern Pakistan canals would receive western waters.

Nehru set out to present India to the world at large as a liberal and democratic state, a model internationalist in a distracted world. His personality made up for India's lack of armed force, and the afterglow of the Gandhian day gave him an initial and inherited moral authority. His two main preoccupations were his relations with the two power blocs and India's general position. But there were also certain overtones which provided an accompaniment to all his actions and occasionally obscured the major themes. One was the unity of geographical India. This led him to demand the incorporation of French and Portuguese India. The French were obliging if slow; the Portuguese were obdurate until Nehru annexed Goa by unilateral action in 1961. Portugal was no doubt provoking and the territory small, but this clear breach of international law seriously damaged the image of India in the world at large. A similar motive led him to back the displacement of the Ranas of Nepal and support an elected ministry. The experiment did not prove a success and the result was a suspicious and resentful neighbour. In Ceylon and Burma the existence of Indian communities caused friction with consequent coolness towards these countries. In fact, by the time of Nehru's death relations were strained with all her immediate neighbours. Another overtone was anti-colonialism. This fitted in well with the atmosphere of the immediate post-war years. It led him to support the Indonesians against the Dutch and the insurgents in Viet-Nam against the Bao Dai régime. The high-water mark of this tendency was the Bandung Conference of Afro-Asian states in 1955, its most strident expression his denunciation of the Suez incident in 1956. This attitude also led him into sympathetic support of the emerging African states. A third overtone was his internationalism which led him to active support of the United Nations. India was in request for concilation and police duties; she played an active part in the Congo crisis of 1960–2 and later in Cyprus. Her record here has been honourable and distinguished.

But Nehru's main concern at first was the relations of the two great power blocs, which in the immediate post-war years seemed poised for a fatal nuclear war. It was in this connection that he devised his most characteristic policy, which is his chief claim to international fame, that of non-alignment. India would stand between the two blocs, taking help from both and siding with neither. She would encourage others to do the same and so create a 'third force' of uncommitted nations stretching from the Atlantic off North Africa to the China Seas. Pakistan's adherence to the Baghdad pact appeared to break the chain but the idea held good until changing circumstances gradually made it irrelevant or unviable. The first of these was the development of the H-bomb. As its potential was realized the prospect of an all-out nuclear war receded and with it the need to be uncommitted to it. Cracks began to appear within the blocs themselves and the world turned to new issues such as the emergence of Africa and the resurgence of China. Nehru was successful in holding the balance between Russia and America but found the additional weight of China too much for him.

Nehru's relations with China are linked with his Asianism, for he saw himself at first as the leader of a new Asia giving light to the rest of the world. When it was clear that China had acquired a strong dynamic government in the Communist régime of Mao Tse-tung and Chou En Lai, he changed the concept from leadership to partnership. For a time he strove to keep China and Russia in balance, but as their divergence increased the difficulty became too great. He had initial success wiht mutual visits and the formulation of the *Panch Shila* or Five Principles of co-existence. His policy received a first jolt when his protests at British action at Suez proved louder than those against the simultaneous Russian action against Hungary. A turning-point came in 1959 when the Chinese changed their policy from controlling Tibet to ruling it and the Dalai Lama fled to India. Indian sympathy welled up for a Buddhist leader whose religion was close to Hinduism, and Chinese suspicion of India's Western links increased. There followed the dispute over the Chinese road to Sinkiang which ran through a portion of land claimed by India as part of Kashmir, disputes over the McMahon line, and finally the Sino-Indian hostilities of 1962. Indian international prestige suffered severely. China had asserted her supremacy in Asia. Though Nehru never renounced non-alignment it was clear that both this policy and that of Asianism no longer had substance. He was still groping for alternatives when death overtook him in May 1964.

14

Pakistan—Jinnah to Ayub

THE RECORD OF PAKISTAN IN THE EARLY YEARS was simpler because the country was smaller, but in its own way was no less dramatic. Here too, refugees loomed large and assassination stalked. Pakistan started with abounding enthusiasm and more than six millions of refugees. Nearly one man in five in West Pakistan was a refugee. The problem, which in India was local in the north and east, in Pakistan was national. The second problem was the integration of East and West Pakistan, separated by a thousand miles of land and more than two thousand miles of ocean and possessing no common characteristics save religion and fear of India. The third pressing problem was that of Kashmir, which, as in the case of the refugees, assumed larger proportions than in India. To the central and south Indian, Kashmir was a tiresome hindrance to the tasks of nation-building; to the Pakistani it was a vital national concern. Beyond and behind all this lay the fact that Pakistan was a new country with its people untried in statecraft; united so far only by an enthusiastic faith in a religion and a way of life and a determination not to be ruled by Hindus. On paper it appeared to be a ramshackle empire; could faith and enthusiasm alone weld it into an indivisible whole?

The Muslim League leader, Mohammad Ali Jinnah, now acclaimed *Qaid-i-Azam* or great leader, became Governor-General and appointed his deputy, Liaquat Ali Khan, as Prime Minister. The seceding portion of the Constituent Assembly met at Karachi, which became the national capital. Provincial administrations were set up and the accession of Muslim States within the Pakistan orbit received. Without records or precedents and short of everything but zeal, the new Government set to work with a will. The immediate problem to be dealt with was that of the refugees. At first this seemed more intractable in Pakistan than in India.

148

The number of refugees who entered West Pakistan (reckoned by the Pakistan Government at six and a half millions)[1] exceeded those who left it by a million. The population of West Pakistan was therefore not only diversified, but overcrowded. There was, moreover, only a skeleton administration to deal with it. Nevertheless, on the whole, the refugees settled down more quickly in Pakistan than in India. In the first place their former holdings in India were, in general, smaller than the corresponding Sikh holdings in the West Punjab. More refugees could therefore be accommodated in the same area without any sense of injustice. Secondly, irrigation schemes such as those of Sukkur and the Thal desert were still in the stage of development. Fresh land was therefore available for surplus refugees and for those landless peasants who had formerly found a livelihood as day labourers for mainly Sikh famers. For some time life was necessarily dislocated in the West Punjab, and politically this led to suspension of responsible government, but the province returned to normal more quickly and with less travial than its neighbour over the border.

The next problem was that of unification and integration. In West Pakistan, Punjabis, Pathans, Sindhis, and Baluchis had never been particularly easy bedfellows quite apart from the major problem of the relations of East and West 'Wings'. Neither the Punjab nor Sind escaped some faction and dissension, but the Central Government treated both with a firm hand.

In general it can be said that the new patriotism and fear of foreign interference at first proved stronger than the old factionalism, belying the fears of those who thought that Muslims could never work together for long. The Frontier Province proved unexpectedly stable under the leadership of Khan Abdul Qayyum Khan. The new-found unity was demonstrated in the two crises of the death of the *Qaid-i-Azam* in 1948 and the murder of Liaquat Ali Khan in 1951. The Government survived without mishap. But from this time a change occurred. The new Prime Minister, Khwaja Nazim-ud-din, was amiable but ineffective. The economic situation worsened with the fall of world prices of jute and cotton, making it difficult to finance imports for development. No national hero remained to whom the nation could look as a founder-father. Instead some strong personalities like Governor-General Ghulam Mohammad struggled for control, while lesser lights began to jostle for position as in irresponsible pre-partition days. East Pakistan continued to be jealous of West and vented its feelings in the overthrow of its

[1] Symonds, R., *The Making of Pakistan*, p. 83.

Muslim League ministry in 1954. Ineptitude and intrigue precipitated serious riots in Lahore in 1953. In the seven years from Liaquat's murder there were six federal ministries, a protracted constitutional wrangle, a dissolution of the Constituent Assembly, and the formation of new parties around prominent personalities. Unlike the Congress in India the Muslim League became only one group of several. Some positive achievements, however, emerged. The Constitution was at length completed and Pakistan became a republic, though still a member of the Commonwealth. The old provinces and Princely States in the west were merged to form with East Bengal the two units of East and West Pakistan, which had equal representation in the federal legislature.

Nevertheless the country was distracted by disharmony between East and West Pakistan, by local jealousies within the west between Punjabi, Sindhi, Pathan, and so on, by economic troubles, and by the ideological dilemma of her relationship to Islam. Apart from fear of India or, as a Pakistani would put it, of Hindu domination, Islam was the only bond uniting the various regional units. But what sort of Islam? Here the rural masses and the bulk of the *ulema* or religious leaders found themselves at variance with the very small Westernized urban class. The former were traditionalist, and suspicious of everything that came from the West except money. They were literal and dogmatic in their interpretation of the Koran and the traditions of the Prophet or *Hadith*. The latter were educated in English and had imbibed, along with a taste for Western machines and luxuries, liberal political and ethical ideas. Beneath a general allegiance to Islam they leaned towards a secular society based on liberal individualism. These views were to the orthodox *maulana* heresy. But at the same time the English-educated class realized that the state could not hold together without Islam; they were therefore not only at variance with the orthodox majority but divided in their own minds. There was a further source of confusion. Along with Western ideas of nationalism they had imbibed a belief in a British type of responsible parliamentary government as the ultimate expression of democracy. They clung to this belief in spite of its patent failure to work. The masses, on the other hand, while having a broadly democratic view, preserved their traditional liking for the strong man who would give them vigorous and paternal leadership. He must work for their good and he must, broadly speaking, be their choice; given these two conditions they preferred a single leader giving intelligible orders to committees or juntas or parliaments or sets of rules.

In the economic sphere the progress of Pakistan was at first unexpectedly rapid. At the time of partition, there were many who thought that a country without heavy industry, and with two widely separated portions whose economics were not complementary, had little hope of prosperity or even survival. The interim budget for the first six months of independence showed a deficit of eighteen million pounds. But a number of factors operated in Pakistan's favour. She was found to be nearly self-supporting in rice (the staple diet of the East 'Wing') and rather more than self-supporting in wheat (the staple diet of the West 'Wing'). Though she had little in the way of mineral wealth or heavy industry, she possessed in jute and cotton two cash crops which were in world demand and produced a favourable overall balance of payments. The strength thus acquired enabled Pakistan to refrain from devaluation in September 1948, and thus placed her in a still more favourable bargaining position. In addition large areas in Sind were still available for irrigation, and the Lower Sind Barrage was in course of construction and was expected by 1953–4 to bring a further 2,700,000 acres under cultivation. Nearly half the federal budget was spent on defence, but there nevertheless remained a surplus for capital development and for improving the general standard of life. As in the political sphere, an abrupt change occurred after 1951. The fall in world jute and cotton prices affected the purchasing power of the Pakistani rupee, and heavy imports in the interests of rapid development produced rising prices, discontent, and the devaluation of the rupee to the Indian level. Economic as well as political forces played their part in the Punjab disturbances of 1953 and the widespread unrest thereafter. An improvement began with the launching of the first of the Pakistan five-year plans in 1955, which will be dealt with later.

By the autumn of 1958 the cup of faction and irresponsibility was ready to overflow. The prospect of elections under the newly promulgated constitution produced a fever of manoeuvre, intrigue, and changing of sides. In October of that year President Iskander Mirza dismissed the parliamentary ministry of Feroz Khan Noon at the call of the Commander-in-Chief, General Ayub Khan, and a group of generals, and authorized him to take over the government. Almost Ayub's first act was to dispense with the President himself. A military dictatorship was set up by a bloodless revolution.

There is no doubt that general relief was felt throughout the country at this intervention. The new Government acted with speed. With the sanction of martial law a vigorous attack was made on profiteering, corruption, and inefficiency. Prominent politicians were faced with the alternatives of facing public inquiries with probable prosecution or retiring from public life. Inevitably there was some military heavy-handedness and crudity but the general effect of these activities of the first few months was that of a welcome purge. The new leader then set himself to deal with the most urgent outstanding problems. The first of these was that of the refugees. Many thousands had never been absorbed into the economy; shanty towns of destitutes had grown up round the principal cities; in Karachi itself there were said to be 120,000 destitute families. By the end of 1959 the back of this problem was broken and the refugees were being housed in newly built and sanitary suburbs. This integration with the general community was the first major achievement of the régime.

The second was the attack on the great landed estates of West Pakistan. Here feudalism was still a living force. Six per cent of the landlords held twenty per cent of the whole cultivable area. They used their social influence and economic power, like English landlords in the eighteenth century, to control the votes of their tenants. But unlike their English analogues they were neither improving landlords nor enlightened public men. Their eyes were fixed on the past. They did not see themselves as the natural leaders of a great national expansion or regeneration; rather they sought power for the sake of power and the personal satisfaction its exercise gave them. Their general influence was therefore reactionary and corrupting and their presence in the legislatures a poison in the body politic. During 1959 their estates were broken up by a series of ordinances. Maximum holdings were reduced to 500 acres of irrigated or 1,000 acres of unirrigated land, the rest being offered to the cultivating tenants at twenty-five years' purchase. Six thousand landowners were affected; over two million acres changed hands, and 150,000 tenants became proprietors. The larger landowners suffered loss, though many had taken precautionary measures beforehand. But the measure was neither revolutionary nor even very drastic. In effect it replaced a small feudal-minded aristocracy with a much larger but still small class of landed gentry and yeomen farmers. The measure carried with it the prospect of improved farming, larger crops, and a more contented peasantry. In political terms it provided a new class of substantial people with a stake in the soil and forward-looking views who, it was hoped, would add an element of stability and responsibility to Pakistan.

We must now turn to the new state structure. Soon after his accession to power the new President announced his determination to hand authority back to the civil power at an early date. In view of contemporary precept and practice of dictators in general, not everyone took these expressions of intention seriously. Nevertheless, just a year after his accession to power, the President announced his new scheme of Basic Democracy. The first stage was carried through in the winter of 1959–60, General Ayub being confirmed as President by ninety-five per cent of the votes cast by the new eighty thousand basic democrats. Further study and discussion led to the completion of the constitution which was promulgated by the President on 1 March 1962.

The constitution may be said to rest on the twin pillars of popular participation and of a strong, popularly based executive. It seeks to take from each according to his ability in a realistic way; by realism is meant the conviction that democratic processes must be adjusted to the fact that eighty per cent of the population are illiterate. The ploughman and the woman at the well are in no position to decide the fate of empires, but they are both capable and entitled to help in the affairs of their village and district. The principle was active participation by all at the local level, delegation of authority to a trusted leader at the national level. Units of about a thousand adults elected a representative who became a basic democrat. He had two functions. On the one hand he sat with up to a dozen others on a union council. This in turn would elect representatives to the sub-district, the district, the divisional, and finally the 'wing' or provincial council. The basic democrat's second function was to be an elector for the national legislature and the Presidency itself. The Presidency and legislature would thus be in the hands of about eighty thousand electors each chosen by about a thousand adult persons. This exhibited indirect election on the soviet model, without the intervention of a party to control the elections.

At the centre power was distributed on the federal plan. East and West Pakistan formed the two 'wings' of the federal structure, with equal and considerable powers, for it was the principle that what could be done at a local or provincial level should be done. The principle of equality was emphasized by the provision that the Legislature should oscillate between Islamabad in the west and Dacca in the east. The federal centre had a separate list of powers, but was further armed with a 'concurrent' list of subjects on which it could override the wings in the national interest. The executive itself was in the hands of the President, to be separately elected for five years on the American model, the electors being the basic democrats. The President was not responsible to parliament but appointed ministers directly responsible to himself as in America. They could address the Assembly but were not to be members of it. The Assembly exercised the legislative function but the President had a veto which could only be overridden by three-fourths of its number. In that case he could hold a referendum or else dissolve the Assembly and himself seek re-election. In finance the Assembly voted all fresh taxes, but could not rescind them without the President's consent. The old device of failing to pass the budget could only block fresh taxation and not bring the whole administration to a halt.

Finally, deference was paid to Islamic principles by the declaration that Pakistan was 'an ideological state' and the setting up of a Council of Islamic Ideology to advise on legislation. How far this represents an attempt to harness the religious leaders, still influential with the masses, to the processes of a modern state, or a chaining of the state to traditional ideology has yet to be seen.

At the first elections, to the general surprise, many of the old and apparently discredited politicians re-emerged as members of the provincial and central legislatures. It would seem that the basic democrats, when looking for provincial and central candidates, often preferred the 'devil that they knew' to the devil they did not. These men lost no time in attempting a return to the old ways, but they found that while they could speak for themselves they could no longer influence other members by hopes of office, because they had none to give, or by bribes and threats, because the new members in general were less venal and more independent than before. They also found a President of determination in possession of all the levers of power, and with no inclination to part with them. There were, in fact, some months of uncertainty while the President pondered how far he could go in satisfying old parliamentary longings without sapping the bases of his own power. In the upshot, apart from the substitution of direct election by basic democrats for indirect election of the provincial assemblies, the system remained substantially intact. The chief casualties were setbacks in university reform and in the project for legal reform. The nascent opposition broke up and the only sign of overt authoritarianism has been a rather strict handling of the Press. The President at first stood apart from party. But he later threw in his lot with a reorganized Muslim League. Both these lines of toughness with politicians and patronage of party seem to have paid off in the Presidential and Assembly elections of 1964–5. The opposition, unable to agree on a policy, united on the candidature of the late founder's aged sister, Miss Fatima Jinnah. In spite of the magic of her name President Ayub won a resounding victory, made the more impressive by the fact that he secured a majority in East as well as West Pakistan.

The first seven years of Ayub's rule were a period of rapid progress. The vital subjects of administration, such as land reform, irrigation, transport, and industrial development, were placed under boards directly responsible to the President. Sanctioned plans and agreed policies could then be administered on a long-term basis without the hazards of annual budget cuts or changes of ministry. The period saw the various irrigation schemes, the settling of the Indus waters dispute with the help of the World Bank, and the development of the Sui gas supply near the Baluchi border. Planning as such began in 1955 with the launching of the first five-year plan, but the new régime imparted a new vigour to its execution. The first five-year plan aimed at using agricultural surpluses to build up the infant manufacturing industry, which in 1950 accounted for only 1.4 per cent of the gross national product. The plan had considerable success in this respect but it left the countryside static and apathetic. The second five-year plan aimed at the stimulation of agriculture by the removal of controls and the use of capital for fertilizers, tractors, tube wells, etc., while continuing the support of industry. This plan as a whole was a great success so that it could be said that while in India in those years population was catching up with production, in Pakistan production was outstripping population. Prosperity was growing, and what was more, it was felt to be growing. There was a feeling of movement in the air. From this vantage-point a third and much more ambitious plan was launched in May 1965, aiming at an increase in production of 37 per cent and of the *per capita* income of 25 per cent. But within months the Kashmir conflict supervened and it now remains to be seen how much of this new production will be syphoned away into armaments.

Foreign affairs were mainly concerned with the Commonwealth, Kashmir, Afghanistan, and the Islamic world. Pakistan showed no wish to leave the Commonwealth; the warmth of her feeling was shown by the free employment of Englishmen in both the civil and military services and the welcome extended to them in other walks of life. If there were periodical suspicions of British partiality in Indo-Pakistani disputes, these never clouded personal or seriously prejudiced official relations. While Pakistan remained a member of the Commonwealth, she also considered herself, as it were, a Dominion of the Islamic commonwealth or brotherhood. She was as independent in relation to the one as to the other, but she had, as it were, a special concern for Islamic as well as for Commonwealth affairs. Under the guidance of the talented Foreign Minister, Sir Zafarullah Khan, she played a friendly and active role in the complexities of Middle Eastern politics, in the tangled affairs of the Arab

League, and in the disputes of Britain with Persia and Egypt. Pakistan found her international feet with unexpected speed, but later her influence was restricted in general by the known weakness of her government at home, and in the Islamic world by the anti-Western policy of Egypt and her Arab friends.

A major shift of policy came in 1954. The rather nominal non-involvement of policy of Liaquat's time was then exchanged for a definite commitment for military aid with the United States, which was later allowed to use air bases. This agreement was preceded by a treaty with Turkey and succeeded by Pakistan membership of both the South East Asia Treaty Organization (SEATO) and the Baghdad Pact (CENTO). Pakistan thus went squarely into the Western camp. The great advantage of this move was the sense of security it gave, not only from India, but also from Russia and a Russian-aided Afghanistan. One untoward result was the U.2 incident of 1959. But more serious was the resentment of India, who interpreted American aid to Pakistan as a threat to herself. A further realignment of policy took place with the rise of Chinese interest in the Indian sub-continent and the sudden clash with India in late 1962. Then India asked for and received military aid from both the United States and Britain. Pakistani pleasure at the Indian discomfiture was unwise; it was succeeded by indignation at the granting of American aid on the ground that it implied a threat to Pakistan. The reaction was indeed very similar to that of India in 1954. There followed the Pakistani flirtation with China leading to a frontier demarcation agreement. This in its turn involved complications in the relations with the United States and Russia so that President Ayub found himself unexpectedly treading a diplomatic tight-rope strung over three world powers. The operation was interrupted by the Indo-Pakistan conflict of 1965 which ended with the tragic Tashkent conference.

The cloud which has darkened the diplomatic sky through all these years has been Kashmir. At the moment of independence a standstill agreement was made with the Maharajah while negotiations proceeded. In October 1947 bands of tribesmen, which, in the then state of sentiment and disorganization, Pakistan was powerless to control, irrupted into the state. There followed the Maharajah's accession to India, the arrival of Indian troops in Srinagar, and a civil war between the Kashmir Government and 'Azad' Muslims. In 1948 Pakistan intervened to prevent their extinction and for a time there was danger of a general war with India. With the help of the United Nations wiser counsels prevailed and a cease-fire and truce line was arranged early in 1949. At the time of accession

Nehru offered Kashmir a plebiscite, and Pakistan's policy has been to obtain one. She accepted the proposals of three successive UNO mediators for holding one but on each occasion the Indian Government did not agree. From 1954 a hardening in the situation occurred. Indian resentment at the reception of American aid by Pakistan was expressed in the dropping of talk of a plebiscite and a series of measures towards the full integration of Kashmir with India. The symbol of this change was the imprisonment of the Kashmir leader Sheikh Abdullah, with a brief interlude, from 1953 to 1964. Feelings on the Pakistan side hardened also, especially after a brief reopening of discussion was ended by Nehru's death; tension mounted until the clash of 1965.

Kashmir remains, after Tashkent as before, the outstanding question between the two countries. For India it is one problem of many, to Pakistan it seems to be a matter of life or death. Muslim sentiment continues to be deeply stirred by the spectacle of a mainly Muslim and contiguous area denied, as it believes, the right of self-determination. At the same time not much attention is paid to the possible wishes of the Kashmiris themselves. All the other main causes of dispute between Pakistan and India, such as refugee property and canal waters, have been settled; Kashmir remains the outstanding obstacle to good relations. It has already caused two small wars and done much to cripple the economic development of both countries. It can only be hoped that each side will realize the necessity of a settlement before disaster overtakes them both.

15
Conclusion

INDIA AND PAKISTAN STAND AT a parting of the ways. The political flux of the present is obvious, but the whole argument of this book has been directed to showing that it is not in politics alone that they have entered the valley of decision, but in the larger and more fundamental field of culture. Far more vital than the struggle for independence is the battle for their soul, or rather we should say twin souls, for just as there are now two governments so there are certainly two souls. The argument has sought to show that the real significance of the eighteenth and nineteenth centuries in Indian development is not to be found in the coming of foreigners from overseas and their establishment as the ruling power, but in the entry of Western ideas and principles along with the British and their challenge to the whole of Indian life and thought. The political struggle leading to the eclipse of Indian independence was as nothing compared to the spiritual struggle, on which depended the survival, transformation, or eclipse of Hinduism and Indian Islam. British power was a mere outward panoply, but the ideas which the British brought with them, or, as may more accurately perhaps be said, let loose in the country, set going a ferment in the minds of Indians themselves, where contrary ideas warring against each other generated incalculable forces. Would there be comprehension and absorption, amalgamation into a new compound, or disintegration by stages or in a single mighty explosion? The problem remains, but it is now possible to trace considerable progress towards its solution. India has considered and tried a number of possible answers, from complete acceptance of the West to complete rejection. It has found a solution (referred to in previous chapters as the Hindu-British and Anglo-Islamic syntheses) which has so far seemed to satisfy the Indian craving to receive ideas from the West without breaking the chain of continuity with the past. Those syntheses have been worked out under the pressure of Western criticism and assumption of superiority, as well as of the traditional Hindu-Muslim rivalries. The desire to achieve a solution was sharpened by the spectacle of Western strength and worldly wisdom. Not so much the oppressor's wrong as the proud man's contumely whetted the appetite for change and assimilation. If only India could be even with the West she would sacrifice much and borrow much.

During the last eighteen years the Westward current in both countries has grown in strength, but the question for the future still remains. Will the new synthesis, which has served so well in the years of cultural struggle as an alternative to the complete obliteration of the old or exclusion from the dangerous delights of the modern Westernized world, prove as effective in the coming years of independence and free choice? Is it, in fact, a genuine synthesis, a reconciliation of divergent ideas by means of some inner unifying principle, or is it merely a hotch-potch of contradictory ideas selected by the instinct of self-respect and held together by Western pressure? Is the synthesis a true union of ideas or merely an *ad hoc* redisposition? Have India and Pakistan found a synthesis or only a compromise?

It is not enough to reply to this question that the new outlook has stood the test of a century's struggle and development. Many movements have prospered so long as they were in opposition, so long as the motive of hatred of something else operated more strongly than the conviction of their inherent worth. The hour of success is the testing time of all movements, and the death knell of many. The ideas which inspire them have then to stand on their own merits and are judged for their inner consistency. Thus, the English Puritan movement began to disintegrate from the moment of its political triumph; while in our own day the same thing has happened to liberalism, both political and economic. The development in their full majesty of the papal claims was separated by but a brief span of time from the captivity of the popes in France, and it was at the moment that the world was made safe for democracy that the palpable decline of liberty began. The Indian synthesis cannot, then, be taken at its face value merely because it thrived on opposition; it is necessary to examine it more thoroughly to see if it is a tree standing by its own strength or a creeper clinging to the decaying trunk of another which must ultimately be involved in a common ruin.

This examination must be separate in the case of both Hindus and Muslims, for the adjustment of each to the West has been necessarily different. Taking first the Hindu case, the examination reveals certain paradoxes in the relations of the two cultures. Modern Hindus have adopted the Western idea of equality, and used their acceptance of it as an argument for political equality with the West and for a social equality among themselves. The whole democratic claim postulates a belief in the equality of man, if not in his gifts and powers, then in his significance and place in the community. Not equal ability but equal judgement and value are the axioms of democracy. But this principle meets with a number of resistances in the Hindu body social and conceptual. There are not only such inequalities in fact as that of landlord and tenant, peasant and prince, industrial magnate and factory worker. There are the deep cleaving and fast clinging customs of caste of which only a few of the outer trappings have so far been thrown aside. To open a temple here and there does not make untouchables touchable; to call these people the People of God does not give access to wells; to eat with other castes on occasion or even to disregard the strictest marriage restrictions within caste does not seriously shake the whole mighty edifice of status by birth, of discrimination and hereditary inequality. Behind caste comes the Hindu attitude to women. It is true that the Hindu should regard his mother as a goddess, and all married women as mothers; it is also true that a wife should regard her husband as her god. A Hindu woman has a position in her home in relation to her children and junior women, but she has no position in relation to her husband or society at large. As Plato saw, and the Greeks discovered by experience, equality cannot flourish for long if it is confined to one half of society. Either it must extend its sway or else lose the grip it already holds. Behind these social resistances come the ideas which originally gave them expression, the ideas of *karma* and transmigration. Caste is the outward and visible expression of the phenomenon of transmigration and reincarnation, which is in itself made necessary by the doctrine of *karma*, the inexorable law of moral consequences. That in turn is linked with the whole theory of existence and of the relation of the individual to the universe and reality. The concept of equality is as disturbing to these ideas as the idea of evolution was in the nineteenth century to a belief in a spontaneous and definitive creation, and to the identification of existing moral conceptions with the order of the universe. One or other of these sets of ideas, it would seem, must give way; the Hindu must go further and cease to be a Hindu or draw back and return his Western loans.

Along with equality goes the Western idea of the individual. For the West the individual is a fixed entity living a single (once for all) life, endowed with rights and saddled with obligations. Though no longer regarded as a separate atom whirling in the universe of mankind un-related to others, though linked by instinct, interest, and duty to his fellows so that he is not wholly himself by himself, but only in conjunc-tion with the society to which he belongs, the individual is the mainspring of Western political and social and religious tradition. Personality is supreme, it is the needs of personalities which give rise to rights and duties, and the worth of each personality which is central to both Christian and democratic traditions. This conception is obviously in-fluential in contemporary India, but contrasts sharply with Hindu ideas on the subject. In Europe, personality is something to be developed; in India, something to be shed. It is not only the Buddhist who saw the purpose of life as the extinction of personality in Nirvana (whether this is absorption in the All or dissolution into nothing does not alter the fact of the extinction of the individual); Hinduism also seeks to escape from the chain of rebirth and to find salvation in absorption in the One. For the Hindu, in truth, it is indeed a chain, for it is a succession of lives, each unreal in so far as it is individual and self-conscious and separate. For the West, individuality is a good to be cultivated; for the Hindu, it is an evil to be dissipated. Nor does the contrast cease here. Hindu thought, in consonance with its attitude to the individual, is social in its aspect. The individual is significant only as a member of a group—family, marriage unit, and caste. He only exists for their good and is un-hestitatingly sacrificed for their survival. The individual is not even wholly himself within these groups, for he has a before and after in past and future lives. He is like a time-iceberg; five-sixths of him is sub-merged in past and future. Here again it is difficult to see how the Western conception of personality can be fully accepted without abandon-ing a fundamental Hindu conception.

A third contrast is to be found in the respective Hindu and Western attitudes to the material universe. The West is world-accepting; for it, the universe is real and significant. Hindu thought is world-renouncing; for it, the universe is a dream and an illusion, the sport of the gods. Full acceptance of Western ideas of material progress and concentration upon industrial development, with its implied acceptance of the Western scientific outlook, accords ill with the doctrine of *maya*. Can one kind of view increase in the same set of minds without the other kind of view decreasing? The whole Western scientific outlook, particularly in its extreme (or, as some would say, its logical) form of scientific determinism, which accepts nothing as real which cannot be observed, measured, and confirmed by experiment—seems irreconcilable with the spirit of

Hindu thought. The one element in common is reason, but whereas in the one case it has developed inwards, towards the understanding of being, in the other it has developed outwards, towards the apprehension of external nature.

When we turn to the field of Muslim thought we find a somewhat different picture. Different elements are mixed in different proportions; or, rather, the same Western conceptions are in contact with different Islamic preconceptions. The Western concept of equality finds a Muslim echo in the equality of all believers before God and their fellowship upon earth. All bow before Him in equal humility and all stand together in the congregation of the faithful. The one exception is that of women, whose position in theory, as in present practice, would seem to be inferior. Even the possession of property is severely limited by the doctrines of use and social obligation. The individual, as in the West, is a separate entity, with one life here and now and with a single responsibility to God and society. His goal is personal salvation, and though he may have duties to society, and be organized in groups, he remains the fundamental unit of Muslim thought. He is real and the work of the Creator, whose handiwork also is the universe. Islamic thought, like that of the West, is world-accepting, and therefore the Muslim can be as interested as the Westener in material development without any inner conflict of ideas. Like the Westerner, the Muslim looks outwards rather than inwards, and he is therefore more open than the Hindu to the scientific attitude to life, with its emphasis upon the reality of nature or the external world. He has even affiliations with modern determinism, for the Muslim doctrine of kismet or fate bears a family likeness to its Christian counterpart of predestination. Only in its acceptance of reason as the guide of life has Islam wavered, but here it may be said that the larger and older traditions, inherited through the Arabs from the great Greek thinkers, is on its side. While, therefore, little future can be foreseen for scholastic Muslim thought which made of Islam a religion of authority based on a divinely and verbally inspired book literally interpreted, there seems much less reason than in the case of Hinduism why Indian Islam should not adapt itself to Western modes of thought. It would seem that Islam can adapt itself more easily to the West as has happened in Turkey, or that if disintegration must come it will take rather the form of shedding one skin for another than of a complete transformation.

What then does the future hold in store for the great Hindu culture? Doubts have been expressed above as to the validity of the Hindu-British synthesis conceived by Ram Mohan Roy and now faced with the supreme test of success and autonomy of thought and action. If those doubts are well based, Hinduism is not emerging from its period of trial and conflict, but just entering upon its most acute phase. It may proceed with Westernization in thought and action; it may establish itself as a great modern materially minded power; but it will be at the price of a complete break with the past, at the price of ceasing to be Hindu at all. The penalty of worldly success may be the end of Hinduism. Or it may throw off the evil thing, and retire within itself to a life of abstraction and philosophic detachment from worldly illusion. Hindusim may save its soul at the cost of worldly success. The price of spiritual purity may be material impotence. Perhaps a century will be needed to decide the issue. But this can at least be asserted. The modern Hindu in his present mood will not willingly or consciously accept either solution. There remains the possibility that in his dilemma he will borrow from British practice in other situations and attempt to muddle through. The inner conflict of the coming years will be soul-searing, the sense of frustration and uncertainty acute, but it is at least possible that the combination of spiritual distress, intellectual travail, and external influences may produce in course of time a new civilization altogether, related to both Hinduism and the West but different from either. If Hinduism cannot hope to be the heir of all the ages, she may in the course of time become the Mother of the heir.

Bibliography

General

THE PURPOSE of this list is to make suggestions for further study in the various subjects treated. It is hoped that these books themselves may suggest fresh avenues to further and more exhaustive studies.

For general atmosphere and the 'feel of India' some of the many travellers' descriptions may be suggested. Here is a short list of such books, neither unduly technical, misleading, or inaccessible.

GIBB, H. A. R. *Travels of Ibn Batuta, 1325–1354* (Broadway Travellers), 1929.

KING, SIR L. (ed.) *The Memoirs of Babur*. Oxford, 1921.

MANUCCI, N. (ed. M. L. Irvine). *A Pepys of Moghul India*. 1913.

BERNIER, F. *Travels in the Moghul Empire, 1657–1668* (ed. V. Smith), Oxford, 1934.

SLEEMAN, SIR W. H. *Rambles and Recollections of an Indian Official*. 1844, etc.

Chapters 1–3.—THE COUNTRY AND ITS PROBLEMS

The phase of rapid change following on independence has dated almost all descriptive work in some degree. The last edition (1907) of the *Imperial Gazetteer of India* remains a standard source of information for much of the groundwork of Indian life. The co-operative surveys edited by Sir J. Cumming entitled *Modern India* and *Political India* (Oxford, 1931 and 1932) will be found useful. SIR V. CHIROL'S *India* (Modern World Series, 1926) is a vivid and penetrating study, and there is finally the comprehensive Chatham House work edited by L. S. S. O'Malley, entitled *Modern India and the West* (Oxford, 1941). On the sociological side SIR H. RISLEY'S *The Peoples of India* (1908) is still a standard work, as is W. CROOK'S *Popular Religion and Folklore of Northern India* (1896).

Chapter 4.—HINDUISM

A useful introductory work is *The Legacy of India* edited by G. T. Garratt (Oxford, 1934). To the descriptive works already mentioned may be added J. C. OMAN's *Cults, Customs and Superstitions of India* (1908). An interpretation of Hinduism from a Christian standpoint will be found in J. N. FARQUHAR's *Crown of Hinduism* (1913), and an original Indian view is K. M. PANIKKAR's *Caste and Democracy* and *Hinduism in the Modern World*. The ABBÉ DUBOIS in his *Hindu Manners, Customs and Ceremonies* (3rd ed., Oxford, 1906) gives a vivid description of Hinduism as practised in South India in the early years of the nineteenth century. Its general accuracy is vouched for by Max Müller, and it is valuable as giving a picture of Hinduism in the south when still virtually unaffected by Western influences.

SIR CHARLES ELIOT's *Hinduism and Buddhism* (3 vols., 1921) is useful for the interaction of the two systems. T. RHYS DAVIES's *Buddhist India* ('Stories of the Nations', 1903) is also useful for Buddhism.

For Caste, J. H. HUTTON's *Caste in India* (Cambridge, 1946) is the latest authoritative work. An Indian study on the subject is *Caste and Race in India* (1932) by G. S. GHURYE. SIR S. RADHAKRISHNAN's *Hindu View of Life* (1927) is a useful introduction to Hindu thought. More advanced studies are ALBERT SCHWEITZER's *Indian Thought and its Development* (1936), and MAX MÜLLER's *Six Systems of Indian Philosophy* (1903).

Chapter 5.—ISLAM

H. A. R. GIBB's *Mohammedanism* (Home University Library, 1948) provides an excellent introduction to the subject. A popular exposition from the Christian standpoint is E. BEVAN JONES's *People of the Mosque* (1932). SIR W. MUIR's *Rise, Decline and Fall of the Caliphate* (revised ed. Edinburgh, 1915) is invaluable for origins, as are the works of PHILIP HITTI. SELL's *Faith of Islam* (Trubner Oriental Series, 1907) is a standard description. *The Koran* is available in many translations, of which RODWELL's (Everyman's Library), D. M. SALE's, and MAULANA MOHAMMED ALI's may be mentioned. For reference there is the *Encyclopedia of Religion and Ethics* edited by DR. HASTINGS, R. LEVY's *Social Structure of Islam* (1957), and M. T. TITUS, *Indian Islam* (1930).

Chapters 6 and 7.—HISTORICAL

A standard work of reference is the *Cambridge History of India* (Vols. I and III–VI). Single-volume works are the *Cambridge Shorter History of India* (Cambridge, 1934), and *The Oxford History of India* (3rd ed., 1958). W. H. MORELAND AND A. C. CHATTERJEE's *Short History of India* (4th ed., 1957) is a readable as well as a reliable recent history. A valuable cultural study is H. G. RAWLINSON's *India, a Short Cultural History* (2nd ed., 1943). An original Indian interpretation is provided by K. M. PANIKKAR's *Survey of Indian History* (Bombay, 1947).

For the modern period the following may be recommended:

SPEAR, PERCIVAL. *The Oxford History of Modern India.* 1965.

THOMPSON, E. *The Making of the Indian Princes.* Oxford, 1943

ROBERTS, P. E. *A History of British India.* 3rd ed. Oxford, 1952.

COUPLAND, R. *India, a Restatement.* Oxford, 1944.

Chapters 8, 9 and 10.—THE BRITISH ADMINISTRATION

For further material on the subjects here dealt with, reference may be made to the *Cambridge History of India*, especially Vols. V and VI, *The Oxford History of India*, and the work already cited by P. E. ROBERTS. O'MALLEY's *Modern India and the West*, already mentioned under Chapters 1–3, is useful for the subjects of the remaining chapters.

Here are some further books:

MORELAND, W. H. *India at the Death of Akbar.* 1920.

BUCHANAN, D. H. *Development of Capitalist Enterprise in India.* New York, 1934.

ANSTEY, V. *Economic Development of India.* 3rd ed., 1949.

MATTHAI, J. *Village Communities in British India.* 1915.

DARLING, M. L. *The Punjab Peasant.* 3rd ed., 1932.
Wisdom and Waste in the Punjab Village. Oxford, 1934.

Chapters 11 and 12.—THE INDIAN RESPONSE

The following may be added to the general works already mentioned:

CUNNINGHAM, J. D. *History of the Sikhs.* Ed. H. L. O. Garratt. Oxford, 1918.

FARQUHAR, J. N. *Modern Religious Movements in India.* New York, 1918.

HOME, AMAL. *Ram Mohan Roy, The Man and his Work.* Calcutta, 1933.

HOYLAND, J. S. *Gopal Krishna Gokhale.* Calcutta, 1933.

BANNERJI, S. *A Nation in Making.* Madras, 1925.

GANDHI, M. K. *The Story of my Experiments with Truth.* Ahmedabad, 1927.

NANDA, B. R. *Mahatma Gandhi.* 1959.

NEHRU, J. L. *Autobiography.* 1936.

GRAHAM, G. F. I. *Life and Work of Syed Ahmad Khan.* 1888.

HUSAIN, AZIM. *Fazl-i-Husain,* 1946.

ANDREWS, C. F., and MUKERJI, G. *Rise and Growth of Congress in India.* Calcutta, 1938.

PHILIPS, C. H. *India.* 1949.

IQBAL, SIR M. *Secrets of the Self.* Tr. R. A. Nicholson. 1920.

IQBAL, SIR M. *Reconstruction of Religious Thought in Islam.* 1934.

LUMBY, E. W. R. *Transfer of Power in India.* 1954.

MENON, V. P. *Transfer of Power in India.* Princeton, N.J., 1957.

Chapter 13.—INDIA UNDER NEHRU

The Constitution of India. Delhi, 1951.

AUSTIN, GRANVILLE. *The Indian Constitution.* Oxford, 1966.

MORRIS-JONES, W. H. *Parliament in India.* 1957.

MENON, V. P. *The Integration of the Indian States.* Princeton, 1956.

GRIFFITHS, SIR P. J. *Modern India* (Nations of the Modern World)

BRECHER, MICHAEL. *Nehru.* 1959.

NANDA, B. R. *The Nehrus, Motilal & Jawaharlal.* 1962.

SMITH, D. F. *India as a Secular State.* Princeton, 1963.

ZINKIN, TAYA. *India.* 1965.

Chapter 14.—PAKISTAN, JINNAH TO AYUB

The Constitution of Pakistan. Karachi, 1962.

SYMONDS, R. A. *The Making of Pakistan.* 1950.

QURESHI, I. H. *The Struggle for Pakistan.* Karachi, 1965.

QURESHI, I. H. *The Pakistani Way of Life.* Karachi, 1955.

STEPHENS, IAN. *Pakistan* (Nations of the Modern World). 1963.

VORYS, G. K. VON. *Political Development in Pakistan.* Princeton & London, 1965.

CHOUDHURY, G. W. *Democracy in Pakistan.* Dacca, 1963.

ROSENTHAL, E. I. J. *Islam in the Modern National State.* Cambridge, 1965.

All publications are from London unless otherwise stated.

Index